Osprey Modelling • 37

Modelling the Tiger I

G Edmundson, D Ned, D Parker, D Thompson & S van Beveren

Consultant editor Robert Oehler • *Series editors* Marcus Cowper and Nikolai Bogdanovic

First published in 2007 by Osprey Publishing
Midland House, West Way, Botley, Oxford OX2 0PH, UK
443 Park Avenue South, New York, NY 10016, USA
E-mail: info@ospreypublishing.com

ISBN 978 1 84603 170 0

Page layout by Servis Filmsetting Ltd, Manchester, UK
Typeset in Monotype Gill Sans and ITC Stone Serif
Index by Alan Thatcher
Originated by United Graphics Pte Ltd, Singapore
Printed and bound in China through Bookbuilders

07 08 09 10 11 10 9 8 7 6 5 4 3 2 1

A CIP catalogue record for this book is available from the British Library.

FOR A CATALOGUE OF ALL BOOKS PUBLISHED BY OSPREY MILITARY AND AVIATION PLEASE CONTACT:

NORTH AMERICA
Osprey Direct, C/O Random House Distribution Center, 400 Hahn Road, Westminster, MD 21157, USA
E-mail: info@ospreydirect.com

ALL OTHER REGIONS
Osprey Direct UK, P.O. Box 140 Wellingborough, Northants, NN8 2FA, UK
E-mail: info@ospreydirect.co.uk

www.ospreypublishing.com

Photographic credits

Unless otherwise indicated, the authors took all the photographs in this work.

Acknowledgments

Gary Edmundson
I'd like to thank the following individuals for their help and generosity in the preparation of this book: Mr Bill Wiseman of WWII Productions; Mr Freddie Leung of Dragon Models Ltd; Adam Wilder of SIN Industries, part of MIG Productions; and Jon Tamkin of Mission Models.

Steve van Beveren
I would like to thank my wife Mary and my two children, Anja and Erich, for their support while working on my contribution to this book. Thanks must also go to my good friends Gary Edmundson, for his help in the preparation of the text and his encouragement while building the model, and Tom Cockle for his advice on what 'Tropen' scheme colours to use. Acknowledgement also goes to the following people and companies for their help and generosity: C. K. Tsang of Dragon Models for supplying the Cyber-Hobby kit; Woody Vondracek for supplying the dry transfers of the vehicle numbers and *Balkenkreuz*; Bill Wiseman of WWII Productions for the Early Tiger I tracks; Aber for the Initial Tiger I etched detail set and the aluminium (and brass) barrel set; Voyager Models for the gun cleaning rod and two cables set.

David Parker
I want to thank my best friend and wife, Christine. Without her encouragement, support and understanding this project may not have been completed. I spent far too many hours shut away folding tiny bits of photo-etch as this model turned out to be a bigger project than I had ever anticipated and throughout it all Christine's support was unstinting. I would also like to thank Jim Sullivan of S&T Products for supplying a set of his excellent replacement tracks for this project.

Dinesh Ned
My sincere thanks to Bernard Cher of The M Workshop for the photography and Sudhesh Nair for assistance with the decals and weathering.

Darren Thompson
Firstly, I'd like to thank Marcus Cowper for inviting me to contribute to this book, particularly alongside such illustrious and well-respected company, also, for his encouragement when the progress was slow.
Thanks must also go to my good friends at my local club, Torbay Military Modelling Society, for the loan of reference material and their honest, constructive critique.
Finally and most importantly, I'd like to thank and dedicate my work to my wonderful wife, Alison, for whose constant love, support and encouragement, I will always be indebted.

Contents

Introduction

Arguably the most famous tank of World War II, Germany's Tiger I tank has been one of the most popular subjects of modellers for many years. Developed as a breakthrough weapon, combining thick armour and a lethal 88mm gun, the Tiger I became a feared adversary for the Allies who faced it in North Africa, Italy and on both the Eastern and Western fronts. The Tiger's production run went from July 1942 to August 1944, with 1,354 vehicles completed. Many improvements and modifications took place over that two-year period, including upgrades to the engine, turret and running gear. Stages of the Tiger's development have been categorized as 'initial', 'early', 'mid', 'late' and 'final', but there were numerous overlaps in factory-produced features that make some vehicles difficult to label.

Modelling the Tiger I came into vogue in the early 1970s when Tamiya produced a kit in their new line of 1/35-scale military miniatures, following soon after with a 1/25-scale version with an interior. In the early 1990s Tamiya produced a retooled 1/35-scale kit of a late-production Tiger I that was a quantum leap ahead of the previous offerings with regard to accuracy and detail. Earlier versions of the vehicle were also released after this, and a flood of aftermarket products followed allowing modellers to create very detailed versions of the tank. Academy and AFV Club later released Tiger I kits, with the Academy one featuring an interior. Tamiya's 1/16-scale remote-controlled Tiger I, released in 2000, was an expensive but amazing feat of engineering, which included movement in all directions, a swivelling turret, gun recoil and engine, machine-gun and main gun sounds. Dragon Models Ltd raised the bar in 1/35-scale kits with their release of the initial- and late-production Tiger I in 2005, as well as making a limited production run of their DAK Tiger I through their web sales outlet, Cyber-Hobby. Tamiya and Skybow have since released 1/48-scale kits of the Tiger I. The aftermarket companies have followed with etched-metal and resin detail sets to enhance the finished kits.

This book showcases the work of different authors constructing six different Tiger I models, using a varied approach to each build. Although Dragon kits have been used for each of the 1/35-scale builds, the details and modelling methods shown can be applied to any of the current kits available from other manufacturers. The authors have shown many modifications and techniques during the construction of the kits that range from early to late variants of the Tiger I. The models have been upgraded from the basic kits with many aftermarket items to show the reader the types of products available and how they are applied. These methods, along with some recommended research material, will help the reader complete accurate and detailed models of the Tiger I.

'121', s.Pz.Abt.501, Tunisia 1943 (1/35 scale)

Subject:	*Tiger I '121', s.Pz.Abt.501, Tunisia 1943*
Modeller:	*Steve van Beveren*
Skill level:	*Intermediate*
Base kit:	*Cyber-Hobby Tiger I Initial Production DAK (6286)*
Scale:	*1/35*
Additional detailing sets used:	*Aber Tiger I Initial Production (35177); Aber Tiger I Early Barrel (35L26); WWII Productions Tiger I Early Tracks (35027); Modelpoint MG-34 Machine Gun Barrel (35100); Voyager Model Cleaning Rods for Tiger I (ME-A054); Karaya Tow Cable Wire*

Introduction

Some of the more interesting versions of the early Tiger I were the ones issued to schwere Panzer-Abteilung 501, which arrived in Tunisia at the beginning of December 1942. Their vehicles had unique headlight mounts, spare track stowage, fenders and rear mudflaps. One of the vehicles photographed during this period was No. 121, which was eventually put out of action on 1 January 1943 near Kairouan. There are very good pictures of this vehicle in both Thomas Jentz's *Tigers at the Front* (Schiffer Publishing, 2001) and Wolfgang Schneider's *Tigers in Combat* (Fedorowicz Publishing, 1994).

Construction

Over the past few years Dragon Models Ltd (DML) has started releasing limited-edition kits through their own online hobby shop called Cyber-Hobby, including the Tiger I Initial DAK (6286). Out of the box this kit has all the required

Schwere Panzer-Abteilung 501 began to arrived in Tunisia with their Tiger Is from December 1942

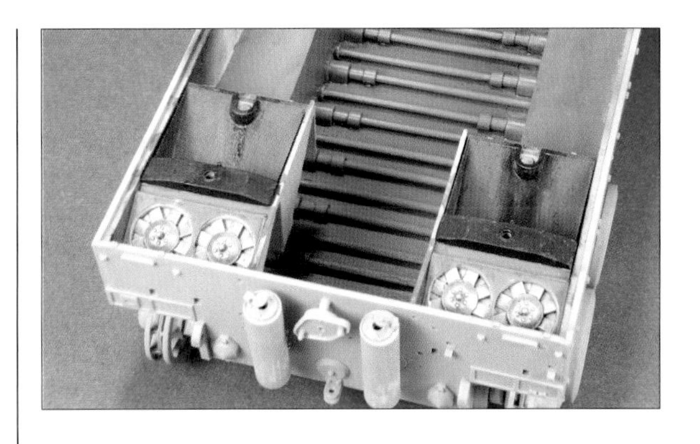

The radiator and fuel tanks once painted and weathered fill the area under the grilles nicely.

Care was taken to ensure a proper fit between the upper and lower hulls.

components to make one of three well-known Tunisian Tiger Is – vehicles 112, 141 and 142. It also comes with numerous photo-etch parts, an aluminium barrel, brass rounds and individual link tracks called 'Magic Tracks'. These tracks are individually packed and ready to assemble, aside from some minor raised ejector-pin marks. While the photo-etch provided in the Cyber-Hobby kit is quite well done I chose to use parts from Aber's excellent set for DML's Initial Tiger I (6252) along with their multi-piece aluminium and brass barrel.

I started construction of the model by cleaning up the roadwheels. After removing them from the sprue and removing the connection points I ran a file perpendicularly across the rubber portion of the wheel. This roughens up the surface and provides some nicks and gouges, which gives the wheels a used and worn look.

The next area I tackled was the partial interior provided in the kit, which consists of the radiator fans and fuel tanks. The fan assembly housing was painted with Vallejo Dark Blue-Grey (904) and the fuel tanks were painted with Floquil Oxide Red enamel. They were given a black-brown wash of oil paints and some fuel stains were made with thinned Tamiya Smoke (X-19). With the interior parts completed the upper and lower hull were glued together. I used some small hobby clamps and Tamiya masking tape to ensure a tight fit between the two and then applied Tamiya's super thin cement.

My attention now turned to the comprehensive etched set for the Tiger I by Aber. I chose to use the front and rear fenders, etched grilles, tool clasps, headlight mounts and smoke discharger parts. I found it helpful to make a small fixture to support the smoke-discharger bracket assembly while I attached the wiring and small chains to the rear of the tube bases.

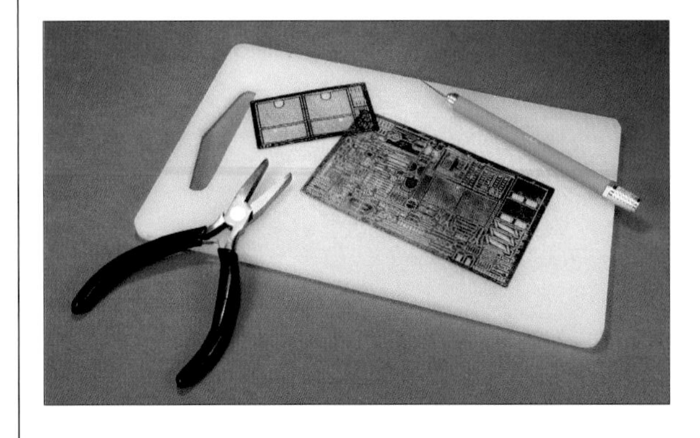

An ordinary kitchen cutting board provides an excellent surface for removing the photo-etch pieces from their carrier frame.

Historex's hexagonal punch and die set was used to make the bolt heads on the side fenders.

Early Tiger Is in Tunisia had extended rear mudflaps so these and the side fenders were scratch built from thin copper sheet.

Two of the unique features of the Tunisian Tigers were the side mudguards and rear mudflap side extensions. On these vehicles the side fenders were made from a small angle attached to the top edge of a flat sheet with a small folded edge along the bottom. Rather than purchase an aftermarket etched set for these parts I decided to make them myself from thin copper sheet. I taped a piece of the copper sheet to my drafting table and, using the sliding ruler, marked out four sets of fenders and the small angle attached to the edge. This would give me two extra sets to work with in the event I wasn't happy with all the pieces made from the first two. Rather than use a pencil to mark out the shapes on the copper sheet I used a small pin mounted in an X-Acto knife handle. The advantages to this are that the lines are easy to see and they cannot get wiped off. It also helps when the pieces need to have bends applied. Once all the parts were marked out they were cut from the sheet with a sharp No. 11 blade. The small angles were formed into their required shape and the flat portion of the fender had its bottom edge folded over. To ensure a secure joint between the fender and the small angle I decided to solder the two parts together. Both parts were individually tinned then clamped together with some small copper clips and heat was applied to both. The advantage to pre-tinning the parts is that you can make sure the two parts are lined up properly before soldering. To get a single curved edge around the rear mudflap extensions, the copper sheet was burnished over a piece of 0.75mm-thick styrene with a rounded corner. Before gluing the soldered side fenders onto the kit each piece was cleaned with lacquer thinner, which removed any flux residue left over from the soldering process. This is important to ensure a good bond, as the cyanoacrylate glue used to attach the fenders to the model will not adhere properly otherwise. The bolt heads for the fenders were made using a Historex hexagonal punch and die set and 0.25mm-thick styrene.

Using the same copper sheet I also made the four small mounting brackets that attached each Feifel air cleaner to the rear hull plate. As all four appeared to be the same I created a small jig that allowed me to form eight identical brackets. The two upper brackets mounted vertically were glued to the air cleaner housing and the lower two horizontally mounted ones were attached to the rear hull plate which allowed me to get a proper fit of the air cleaner. In the photos of '121' I could see that one of the air cleaner hoses was missing from the left air cleaner, so I enlarged the hole in the bottom mounting flange and added the four holes for the missing bolts. I also replaced the thicker kit parts for the hose mounting brackets on the engine deck with parts made from styrene.

A small fixture was made to aid assembling the delicate etched smoke candle dischargers.

Up until June 1943 smoke candle dischargers were mounted on the turret sides.

The completed side fenders were cleaned with a lacquer-based thinner to remove any flux residue before gluing to the hull. This ensures a good bond.

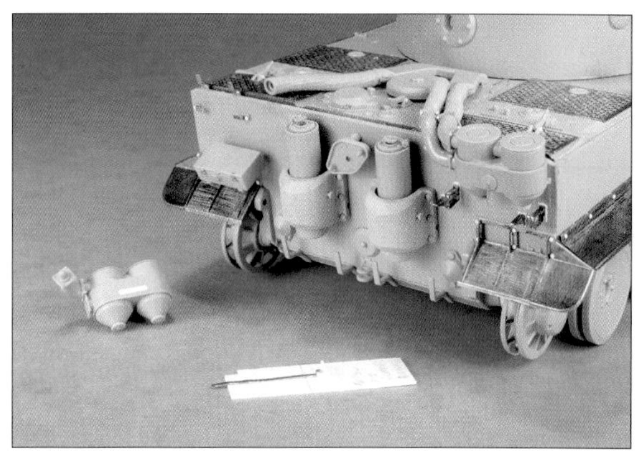

Using sheet styrene a small jig was made to allow multiple Feifel air cleaner mounting brackets to easily be made.

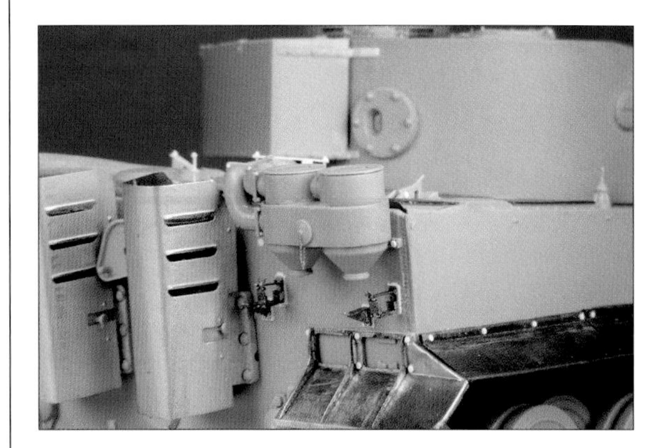

I made the small retaining chains on the air cleaners by cutting a small strip of copper and then twisting it.

Brass wire was used to replace the kit's overly thick plastic handles.

Instead of using the kit's 'Magic Tracks', WWII Productions resin tracks were used since they have open guide horns and don't require gluing.

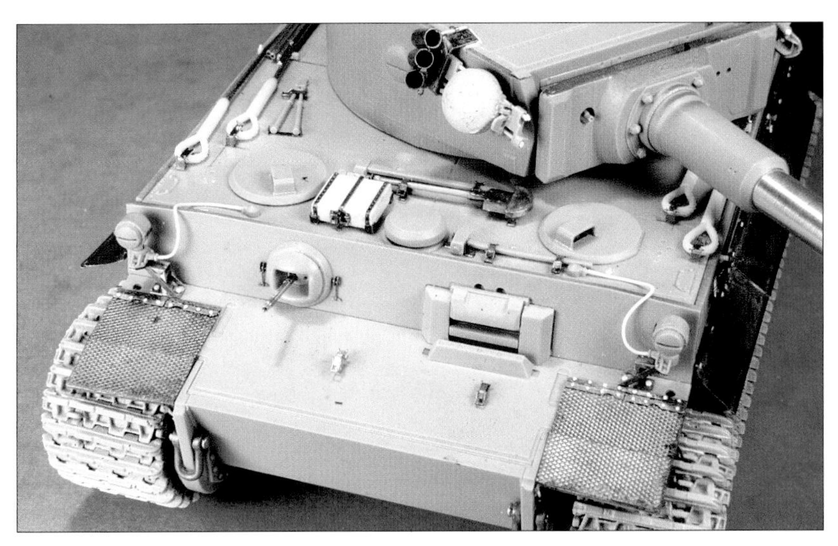

The hull machine-gun cover supplied had its shape reworked with epoxy putty. It was then mounted over the right-hand track link on the turret side.

Voyager's Barrel Cleaning Rod set (ME-A054) for the Tiger I, which includes tow cables, was used minus the brass tow cable wire.

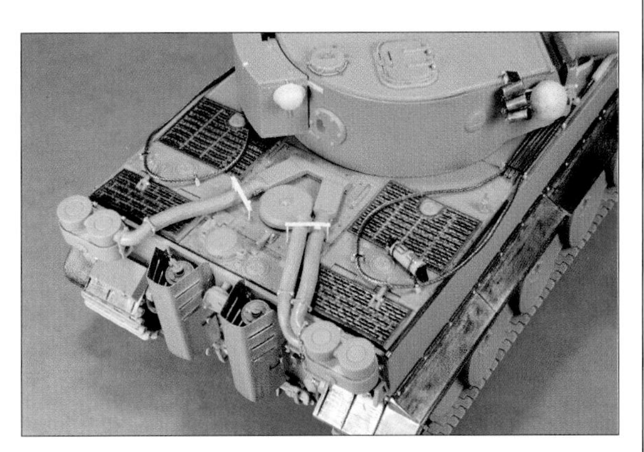

Aber's engine deck screens have a woven mesh appearance.

Tiger Is in Tunisia had unique exhaust guards, which are included in the Cyber-Hobby kit.

Armed with the powerful 8.8cm KwK 36 L/56, the Tiger I was a potent adversary.

The last area to be tackled was the tracks. I decided to use aftermarket tracks manufactured by WWII Productions out of Australia. These are well-detailed resin track links that require minimal clean-up and simply snap together. The two runs of track were completed in about an hour's time.

Karaya brass cables replaced both the tow and track cables supplied in the Voyager's Barrel Cleaning Rod (ME-A054) aftermarket set.

Vallejo Khaki Brown (024) was applied as the basecoat along with Green Brown (030) as the 'Tropen' camouflage.

Painting and weathering

I started by first painting the model with Floquil's Grey Primer, which is an enamel paint and adheres well to both plastic and metal. The model was then lightly pre-shaded using a black-brown colour made by mixing Tamiya's Flat Black (XF-1) and Flat Earth (XF-52). I heavily applied this around the lower hull panel lines. The application of the vehicle's 'Tropen' scheme camouflage was next. After studying the photos of the rebuilt Tiger I at the The Tank Museum, Bovington, UK, and discussing the colours with fellow modelling colleagues I decided to use Vallejo's Model Air paints, specifically Khaki Brown (024) and Green Brown (030). As the 'Tropen' scheme consisted of a somewhat specific ratio of paint colours, care was taken during this part of the painting process to ensure I achieved a 2:1 colour ratio.

Both the turret numbers and the *Balkenkreuz* were applied by using dry transfers from the Archer fine transfer range. These are simply burnished onto the model when there is still a clean surface and then sealed with some clear varnish.

The model was then given a wash using a mixture of black and raw umber oil paints. I prefer to not use an all-over wash as this can significantly alter the base colours. Instead only the lower hull and panel lines received the wash. Once this was dry I airbrushed Tamiya Buff (XF-57) and Flat Earth (XF-52), heavily thinned with isopropyl alcohol, in varying intensities around the lower hull, roadwheels and around objects on the upper hull and glacis. Another light application of dust was created using Humbrol Dark Stone (187) lightly

Thin strips of tape were used to mask off the areas of the track where the roadwheels would run over.

Tamiya Buff (XF-57) and Flat Earth (XF-52) were airbrushed over areas of the kit as the initial application of dust.

Humbrol Dark Stone (187) was drybrushed around the top edges of the vertical plates and then streaked using mineral spirits.

The oil stain on the lower glacis plate was made using a mixture of raw umber oil paint, Humbrol Gloss (035) and Black (021) paints all thinned with mineral spirits.

The cleaning rods were painted Vallejo Buff (976) then lightly drybrushed with Winsor & Newton Raw Umber oil paint.

Up until they were discontinued in October 1943, Feifel air cleaners were mounted on the rear hull plate of the Tiger I.

Paint chips were made using Vallejo German Camouflage Orange Ochre (824) and then partially overpainting these with Vallejo Chocolate Brown (872).

The turret stowage bin was altered to be a slightly different shade of the basecoat by using mineral spirits tinted with yellow oil paint.

Tiger '121' served in Tunisia up until 1 January 1943 when it was put out of action.

drybrushed around the top edges of the vertical plates of the hull and on the top surface of the barrel. Before this paint was fully dry I used mineral spirits to pull it down to create an impression of rain-streaked dust. To add a bit of colour the headlight bases on the upper hull and the flange on the Feifel air cleaner missing the hose were painted with Vallejo Hull Red (985) lightened with Red (70947).

I painted the wood portions of the tools and cleaning rods with Vallejo Buff (976) over which I lightly drybrushed raw umber oil paint and these were both overpainted with Vallejo Satin Varnish (522). This same technique was used on the small wooden box on the rear right-hand fender. The metal portions of the tools and the tow cables were painted with Humbrol Metal-Cote Gunmetal (27004), which can be buffed to have a slight metallic sheen. This same colour was lightly drybrushed around hatch openings and areas of wear. The tow cables then received a dust-coloured wash.

Finally, the tracks were painted with Tamiya German Grey (XF-63) and then randomly sprayed with Tamiya Buff (XF-57) and Flat Earth (XF-52). A mixture of isopropyl alcohol, Gunze Flat Clear (H20) and various colours from the MIG Productions pigments range were then applied to the tread surface of the tracks. This same mixture was applied around the lower hull and under the sponsons. The oil stains on the hull side and lower glacis were made using a mixture of raw umber oil paint, Humbrol Black (021) and Gloss Varnish (035), all thinned with mineral spirits. To finish off the model a very light application of the same pigments used on the tracks was applied around raised areas on the horizontal surfaces.

'321', s.SS.Pz.Abt.101, Normandy 1944 (1/35 scale)

Subject:	*Tiger I '321', 3.Kompanie s.SS.Pz.Abt.101 Normandy, June 1944 (Mid Production, December 1943)*
Modeller:	*Gary Edmundson*
Skill level:	*Intermediate*
Base kit:	*Cyber-Hobby Tiger I Initial Production DAK (6286); Dragon Models Ltd Tiger I Late Production (6253)*
Scale:	*1/35*
Additional detailing sets used:	*WWII Productions Tiger I Mid/Late Track Links (35028); WWII Productions Spare Track and Detail set (35030); Lion Roar Tiger I (Late Version) Metal Mesh Update set (LAM033); Karaya TC Tow Cables; Aber German Tool Clamps (35A93); Royal Model German Fire Extinguisher – WWII (247)*

Introduction

The vehicle modelled in this chapter is an example of a mid-production Tiger I built in December 1943. Vehicles termed 'mid' are typically from the production batches between July 1943 and January 1944, and had the newer turret with cast armour cupola in addition to the rubber-tyred roadwheels. The particular tank featured here served in Normandy with 1.SS 'Leibstandarte' in 3.Kompanie of s.SS.Pz.Abt.101 in June 1944, and its photo is frequently featured in Tiger I reference books.

Lower hull and running gear

As the vehicle would have had the later Maybach HL 240 P45 engine installed, the hull from the DML Tiger I Late Production was used, featuring the correct

Dragon's Tiger I Late Production and Cyber-Hobby's DAK Tiger I were combined to create a mid-production vehicle as used by s.SS.Pz.Abt.101 in Normandy, 1944.

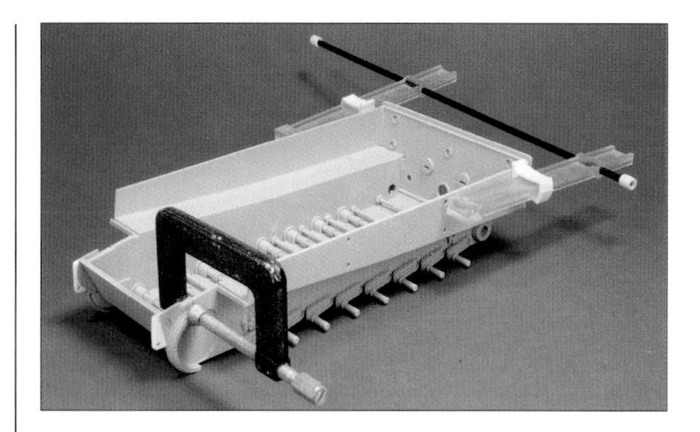

Clamps were used to ensure that the hull parts were glued together tightly.

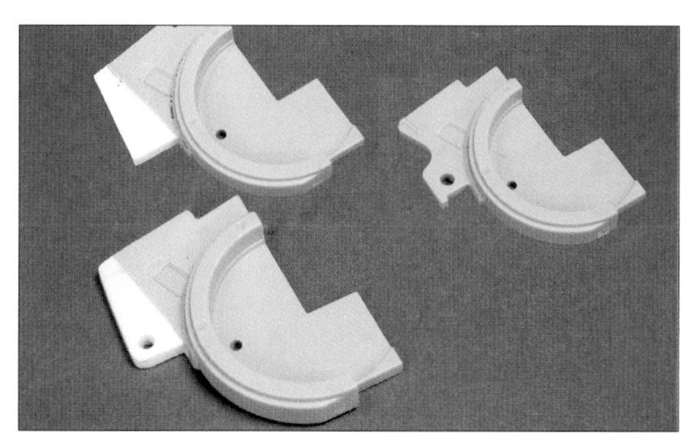

The late-production kit's front towing pintles were modified using .060in. styrene to represent the mid-production's flat style.

access plates on the bottom. The front towing pintle was modified from the kit to represent the earlier style with the flat front. Some .060in. styrene sheet was cut to match scale drawings in Tom Jentz and Hilary Doyle's book *Germany's Tiger Tanks D.W. to Tiger I – Design, Development and Modifications*. The rubber-tyred roadwheels from the DAK Tiger I were glued onto fixed supports. The larger-diameter idler wheels were added onto mounts made adjustable by squeezing the post with a pair of pliers to allow a very tight fit.

WWII Productions Mid/Late Tiger I track links replaced the 'Magic Tracks' supplied in the kit, since they are lacking the hole detail in the guide teeth and front of the link itself. Ninety-six links per side were clicked together, then painted and weathered before installation on the model.

Upper hull

The bullet splash ring for the turret on the DML late-production upper hull (introduced in February 1944) was carefully removed with a flat hobby blade and the area was sanded flat. Locating holes for the axe and pry bar were filled with styrene plugs made by gluing in stretched sprue. After filling the locating holes on the late-production hull top, the tow cable fasteners were re-positioned forward and closer together. The earlier short-tow cable ends were glued onto replacement Karaya copper cables, which were positioned onto the upper hull using cyano glue at each fastener. The kit's fasteners feature nicely moulded wing nuts that were given a half-turn with a pair of tweezers, allowing them a more realistic position.

WWII Productions' tracks replaced the kit's 'Magic Tracks', which did not feature the prominent hole in the guide teeth. The row of spares on the front plate had three blocks of wood jammed between the teeth, replicated with balsa.

Zimmerit

Beginning in August 1943 and continuing until September 1944, *Zimmerit* anti-magnetic paste was applied to Germany's medium and heavy tanks including the Tiger I. The method of application and resulting texture varied between different vehicles. Tiger '321' from s.SS.Pz.Abt.101 featured a typical pattern of *Zimmerit* seen on the vehicles in Normandy with thick lines of texture on the turret and finer lines on the hull and gun mantlet.

To simulate the *Zimmerit*, Aves Apoxie Sculpt putty parts A and B were twisted into manageable lumps about the size of a large pea and spread onto the surface of the model. To make the *Zimmerit* ridged, the surface of the putty was dampened with water and impressed with an appropriately sized screwdriver blade: 4mm for the hull, and 6mm for the turret. Working in small sections at a time, this method took about three hours in total to complete. When dry, the turret *Zimmerit* was sanded down slightly to simulate the appearance of the texture apparent in wartime photos.

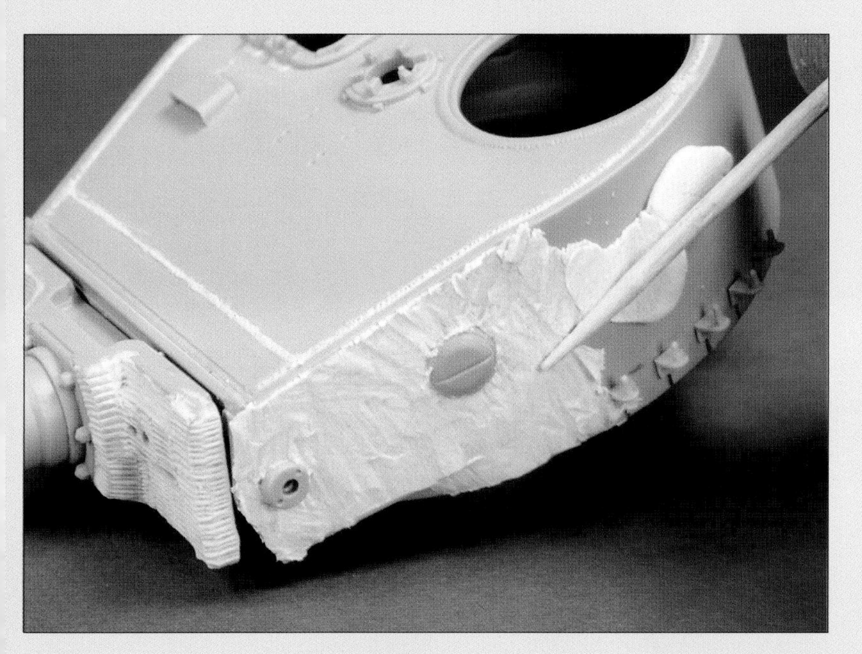

Aves Apoxie Sculpt putty was mixed and then added to the surface using a dampened toothpick. The layer was made as thin as possible, keeping a consistent depth.

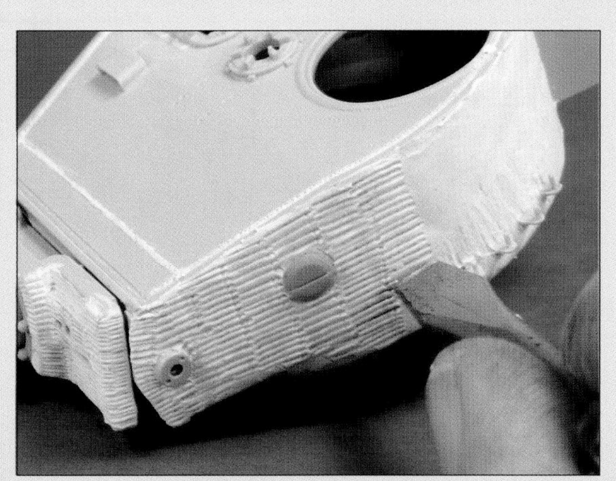

After wetting the surface, a screwdriver blade was used to make the impressions. A large blade was used for the turret, and a smaller size for the hull and mantlet.

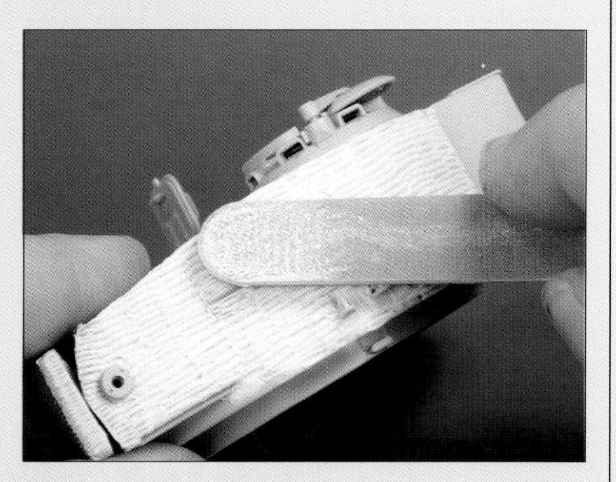

After the putty had dried, a sanding stick was used to slightly flatten the appearance of the turret *Zimmerit*.

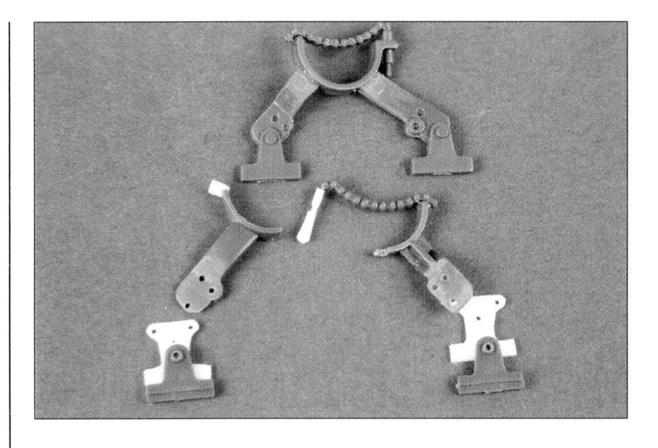

Tamiya's gun travel lock was modified using scraps of styrene card. There are two of these parts contained in each of their initial-, early- and mid-production kits.

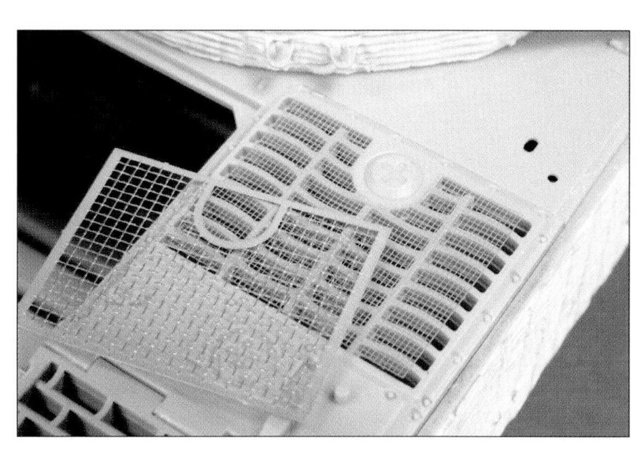

Lion Roar's photo-etched grille set includes the finer mesh that was located beneath the coarser screen on the engine deck cooling air intakes.

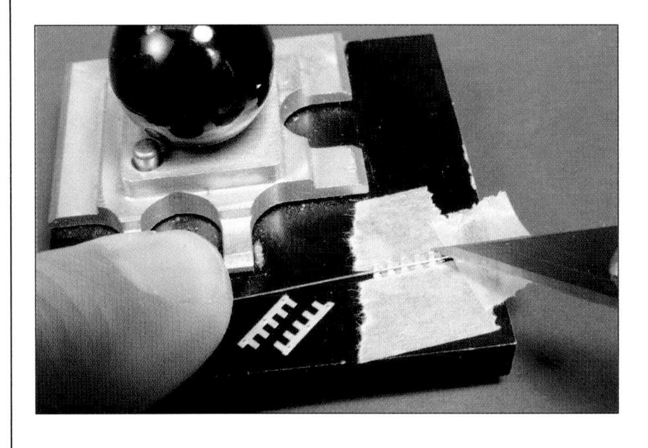

To construct DML's etched-metal front mudguard hinges, the parts were meshed on a flat surface and taped in place to help manipulate them.

After placing thin wire at the apex of the meshed 'fingers', they were folded over using tweezers. The completed hinges were glued to the mudguards with cyano glue.

The kit's gun-cleaning pole sections were replaced by constructing separate ones from .047in.-diameter styrene rod. Five sections were 27.5mm in length, and the sixth was 26.5mm after Doyle's reference drawings in *D.W. to Tiger I*.

DML's late-production Tiger photo-etched brass mudflaps were soldered together. The hinges were taped down to a sturdy base to allow the interlaced fingers to be folded over a piece of thin wire resulting in a workable hinge. The mudflap assembly was then cemented into place using cyano glue. The fasteners for the front of the mudflaps were made from scrap photo-etched runner and styrene. One of these disappeared during the weathering process, so the remaining empty mount was painted to look like it was damaged in action. Unused brackets for a large shovel were added to the glacis plate using Aber's German Tool Clasps Set No. 2.

The rear hull plate from DML's late-production Tiger featuring the access plate below the left exhaust was used. Bolt lugs were added for the exhaust shields and Feifel air cleaner mounts. The lifting lugs for the armoured covers leave a rather hideous gap around the locating hole, so this was filled with Tamiya putty.

A gun travel lock was fitted on Tiger I vehicles from November 1943 until February 1944. Tamiya's initial-, early- and mid-production kits (35227, 35216 and 35194 respectively) each contain two of these parts located on the wheels sprue 'B'. The part is somewhat simplified, and was modified using the factory

The gun's travel lock was cut so as to have the keyed sections at the joint. A styrene handle was added to the locking chain.

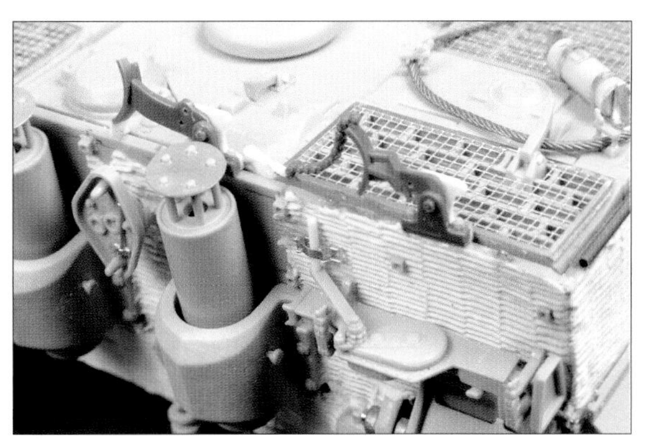

Since the tank was produced in December 1943, it was equipped with the smaller jack, taken from the DAK Tiger I kit. Later models used the heavier 20-ton jack.

illustration found in Jentz and Doyle's *D.W. to Tiger I.* The supports were improved by adding new inner sides with .020in. styrene card, and the mount itself was separated showing a keyed joint by carefully digging it apart with a new No. 11 hobby blade. The locking handle and plate were fashioned from styrene, with the plate set to a more accurate angle.

Lion Roar LAM033 metal mesh for the cooling air intakes provides two layers of etched-metal screen. Finer screen was placed underneath the coarser. The engine hatch dome was the rounded style part P24 with the knob taken from part J13. The engine deck latch hinges had .028in. styrene discs added to the sides that were made from a Waldron punch and die set.

Royal Model's German Tanks Fire Extinguisher – WWII No. 247 – consists of resin cylinders and photo-etched straps and other details, and the later style was used on the model. The straps were pre-bent over 3mm brass tubing, which allowed them to hug their respective locations prior to gluing. The kit-supplied jack from the DAK Tiger was used since the sturdier 20-ton jack was not added to the production run until January 1944.

A crew was constructed using Tristar's tank figures, resin heads, and part of a Show Modelling figure for the commander.

Turret

The turret roof of the late Tiger was modified to have the early loader's hatch frame by filling the hinge cutouts and the hole for the close-defence weapon. The frame was removed from the DAK Tiger I roof plate and glued in place. The loader's hatch was modified to have the handle located centrally, along with the lock mechanism on the inside.

A weld bead was placed across the roof 5mm from the front by scribing a deep line and filling it with putty To change the modelled thickness of the turret roof from 40mm to the earlier 25mm type, the very front lip of the roof plate was removed and the underside edge of the roof was trimmed. This allowed the rooftop to sit flush with the turret walls. The resulting trough around the turret perimeter was filled with putty that was textured to resemble weld bead.

The turret ventilator had six tabs that allowed fasteners for a waterproof cap to be hooked underneath. The kit examples were shaved off and tiny styrene ones added.

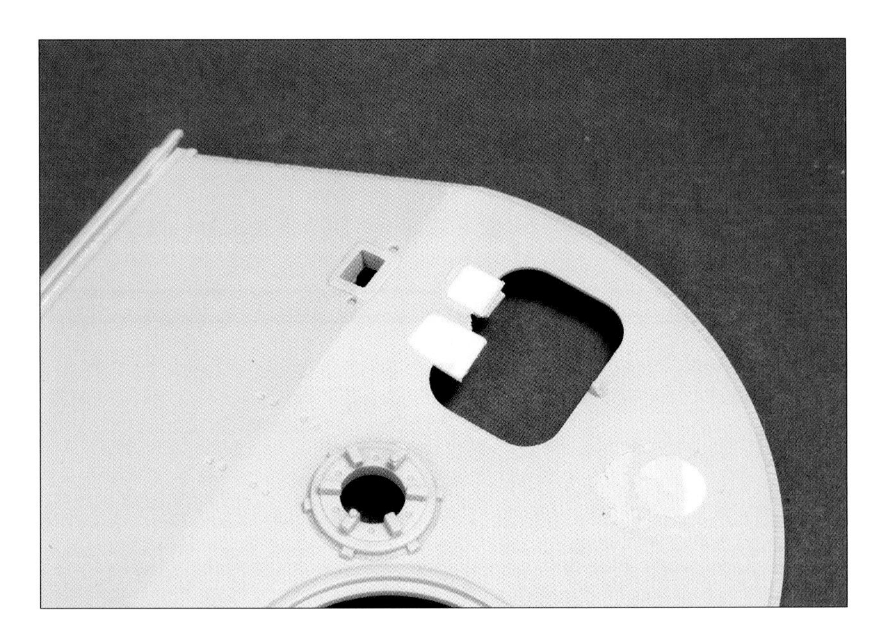

The late-production turret roof had the close-defence weapon hole filled with a styrene plug. To adapt the earlier loader's hatch, the cutouts for the hinge were also filled with styrene. Tamiya putty was applied, and sanded smooth.

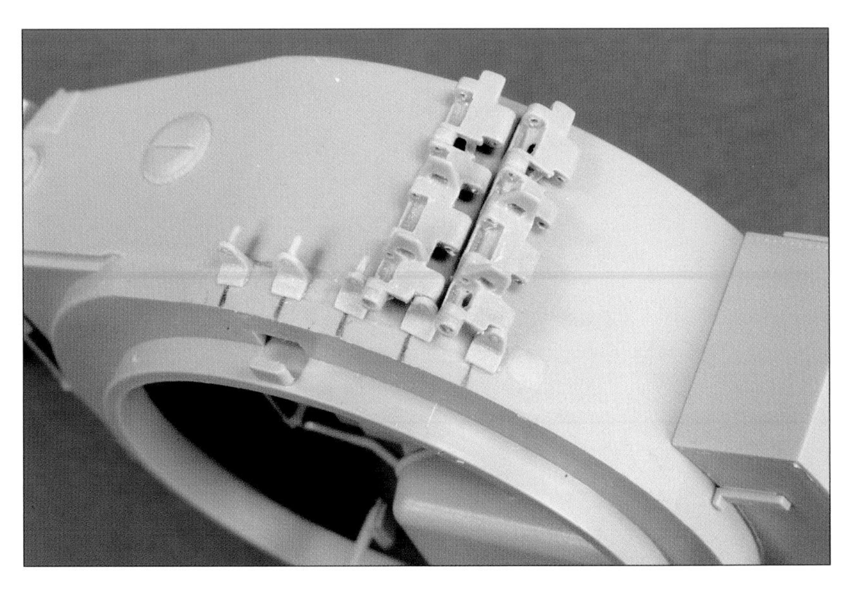

The kit's locators for the spare track links were moved to the left and closer together to match references.

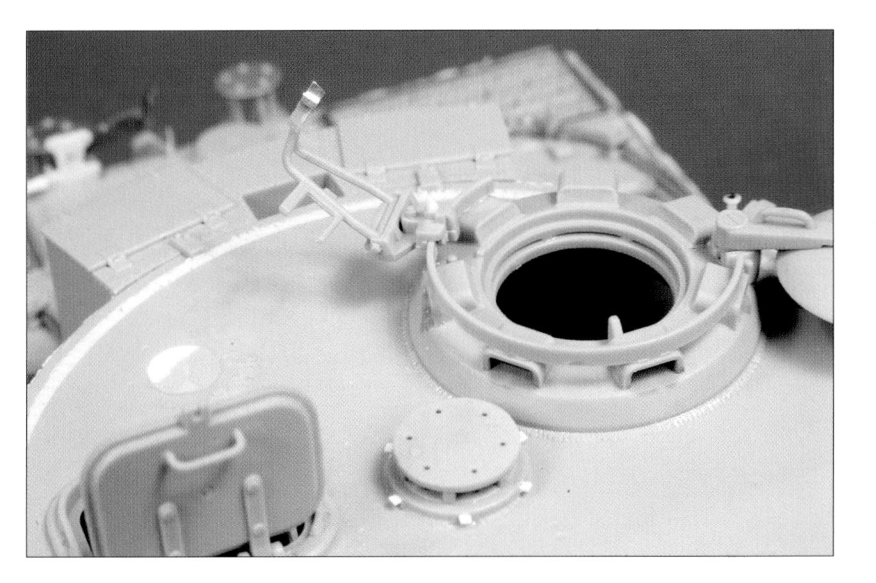

The turret roof of the late-production Tiger I was lowered to represent the 25mm-thick version. The loader's hatch had the earlier frame, with the handle and lock centred.

Painting

The model was painted with the roadwheels glued in place and the tracks done separately. The first step was to airbrush on a coat of dark-brown Floquil lacquer as a primer. This adheres well to the surface of all of the many types of media used to make the model, and provides a pre-shadow to the model that helps with the weathering process later. The lacquer-based paint has to cure for approximately two days before any subsequent colours are applied.

The basecoat of the camouflage was a mixture of Tamiya's Dark Yellow (XF-60) and Desert Yellow (XF-59) in a 4:1 ratio. This was lightly airbrushed on allowing the dark-brown base to remain visible here and there, especially around the running gear. It also served to accentuate the *Zimmerit* texture of

The model was primed with a dark-brown Floquil lacquer mix, and then basecoated in Tamiya's acrylic paint. The model was supported on a file handle that had a wood screw epoxied in the end. This was then threaded into a hole in the bottom of the model.

Camouflage colours of olive green and red brown were sprayed onto the model using thinned Tamiya acrylic paint. By diluting the paint to a 1:4 ratio, a fine demarcation line was achieved.

The blue colour of 3.Kompanie's turret numbers was mixed with Vallejo's acrylic paints and added carefully to the decals taken from the late-production DML kit.

The exhausts were painted a pinkish colour and then spotted with dark brown. Rust-coloured pastel chalk dust was then brushed on, creating the desired effect.

The lower regions of the model were treated to a mix of Hudson & Alan's Mud, water and pastel chalk. To vary the look of the muddy surface, dark-brown watercolour paint was daubed on randomly.

Fuel spills were added to the appropriate areas using Tamiya's Smoke (X-19).

Black pastel chalks were used to create the stains on the exhaust shrouds and covers.

The rear of the vehicle received a heavy spray of dust-coloured Tamiya acrylic paint. The track links were painted with a dirt colour and drybrushed with a mix of silver and steel enamel.

Crew figures had their uniforms picked out in Humbrol enamels after they were primed in black. The heads and faces were primed with tan enamel, and then finished in oils.

the model. The camouflage patches of green and brown were sprayed on with a very dilute mixture of Tamiya acrylics. Olive Green (XF-58) was toned down with a little Field Grey (XF-65), and diluted to about 25 per cent paint to thinner. This gives a very fine demarcation between the lines of colour, as opposed to a messy looking splatter when the paint is too thick.

Decals from the DML Late Tiger were applied to the model, but had to have the appropriate light-blue colour painted onto the clear film for 3.Kompanie, s.SS.Pz.Abt.101. Solvaset was required to soften the decal film and allow it to settle in to the contours of the *Zimmerit* coating. The roadwheels had the visible portion of their tyres painted with Floquil's Weathered Black, which is actually a dark-grey colour. This same paint was used to add paint chips to the vehicle's areas of wear. The tow cables were also painted dark grey, and then drybrushed with silver enamel that had been toned down with raw umber oil paint. As a final touch, the cables were brushed with dirt-coloured chalk pastel dust.

After all of the details had been painted, the model was given a light airbrushing of dirt colour mixed with various Tamiya acrylics: XF-57 Buff, XF-51 Khaki Drab and XF-52 Flat Earth were combined and diluted to about 10 per cent paint to thinner and sprayed over the surface of the model, paying more attention to the lower and rear portions. A wash of raw umber oil paint

The gun barrel was painted dark grey, since it appears quite dark in the wartime photos. A colour photo of Tigers taken during the war showed the darker barrels being grey as opposed to primer red.

The vehicle was given a wash of mineral spirits and thinned raw umber oil paint was added to various areas to enhance detail. The oil paint was also dragged down vertical surfaces to simulate rain streaks.

The model was placed in a small vignette depicting its deployment in Normandy, using a selection of DML figures from various sets, and a resin signpost from MK35. To form the base, Aves Master Mache was mixed with water and acrylic paints, and then spread onto a trophy plaque. The surface of the plaque had been roughened with a course grade of sandpaper to help adhere the groundwork. Dirt, grit and static grass were pushed into the mixture, and Heki's grass mat was added to various areas afterwards.

followed by dampening the surface of the model with mineral spirits and allowing the thinned oils to flow in and around details. The wash was dragged in a downward direction along the fenders and mudguards to give the appearance of rain streaks.

Certain areas of the model were highlighted by gently drybrushing with Humbrol's Khaki Drill enamel. Dirt-coloured chalk pastel dust was brushed onto various areas on the model to break up the monotony of the paint scheme and add a dusty look to the running gear and rear end of the tank.

To give the model some life and size perspective, figurines were placed in the open hatches. Tristar's figure set German Panzer Crew (Normandy 1944) provided three of the tankers, two of which were modified with resin heads. The driver figure was positioned leaning over the sponson, since the hatch was located above this area creating an awkward access for that crewman. A Show Modelling figure provided the body for the tank commander. The figures were painted using oils for the faces and hands, and a mixture of Humbrol enamels and Vallejo acrylics for the camouflaged uniforms.

‘322’, s.Pz.Abt.507, East Prussia, November 1944 (1/35 scale)

Subject:	*Tiger I Late Production, s.Pz.Abt.507, East Prussia, November 1944*
Modeller:	*Dinesh Ned*
Skill level:	*Intermediate*
Base kit:	*Dragon Models Ltd Tiger I Late Production (6253)*
Scale:	*1/35*
Additional detailing sets used:	*Friulmodel Tiger I Mid/Late Tracks (ATL-06); some scratch-built details*

Introduction

Established from the first battalion of Panzer Regiment 3 in May 1943, schwere Panzer-Abteilung 507 saw extensive action on the Eastern Front from spring 1944 onwards. The Tiger I crews of the unit were very fond of attaching additional armour to their vehicles in the form of spare tracks to the turret sides and hull fronts. Having seen a picture Tiger ‘322’ abandoned near Praschnitz after a failed recovery attempt, in *Tigers In Combat Vol. 1* by Wolfgang Schneider (Fedorowicz Publishing, 1994), I knew this was the tank I wanted to model.

DML’s new kit of the steel-wheeled Tiger (6253) proved an admirable starting point for this project. Consisting of about 624 parts moulded in light-grey plastic, the kit also provided a potpourri of other goodies normally associated with aftermarket manufacturers, like clear plastic periscopes, aluminium barrel with spring recoil, turned brass 88mm rounds and empty casings, over 30 assorted metal replacement pieces and notably no fewer than three frets of photo-etch incorporating tool latches and hasps, engine deck mesh grilles and other fine details. While DML did provide individual link ‘Magic Tracks’, these crisply moulded links lacked the lightening holes for the guide horns and had pin-ejector marks on the inside surface of each track, so I opted for a set of white-metal replacements from Friulmodel: (ATL 06) – Late Tiger I/Sturmtiger tracks with cleats. This was the only aftermarket item I needed for this build.

The completed ‘322’.

Lower hull and running gear

I assembled all the running gear, including the smaller 600mm idlers, and attached the final-drive housings and track repositioning plate (B20) in a slightly downward sloping direction.

The tub assembled flawlessly and it was gratifying to see many of the lesser-known welded joints accurately reproduced. The side skirt attachment lugs that come moulded onto the hull side plates were slightly undersized, so I replaced them with ones made from styrene. Since this was a '3-in-1' kit (allowing you to build either a late/final or Befehlswagen variant) Dragon provided a choice of two rear plates and I used the correct one for a late variant.

The Tiger I exceeded the weight limits that its original design stipulated; thus suspension failure was a constant problem throughout its service life. To simulate the low sit of a war-weary Tiger, I cut off the positioning stub at the back of each axle arm and lowered their angle slightly, with a subtle bias towards the rear, since that's where the heavy Maybach power plant sat. Constant checking of alignment while the glue dried ensured that the wheels would sit flush with the ground later on.

The kit also included two finely detailed subassemblies representing the left- and right-hand radiator/fuel tank cells as well as the cooling fans. I assembled them and painted them in primer red, adding a metallic tone to the fan blades by applying graphite from an HB pencil. They were then given a wash of oil paints to highlight detail, lightly drybrushed and then fixed in place. All requisite interior details were assembled and then the hull roof was fixed into place.

Zimmerit

This anti-magnetic mine coating was applied to all German AFVs for about a year, from the autumn of 1943 to autumn 1944. This meant that all 530 Tiger Is with steel wheels would have this feature.

I simulated my *Zimmerit* using Tamiya's two-part epoxy putty and two sizes of small flat-head screwdrivers. I mixed out small amounts of putty and spread it evenly by hand, working one area at a time, dipping my finger periodically in water to overcome the stickiness. After it was spread evenly and thinly, I added ridges with the screwdrivers, using the smaller one for the hull areas, and the bigger one for the turret and mantlet. The pictures I had of Tigers of s.Pz.Abt.507 seemed to indicate that their *Zimmerit* covered the entire hull side plates and did not stop at the side skirts. Once dry, selected areas could be scraped away, either to allow a proper fit for other detail parts to be added on, or simply to replicate battle damage.

The *Zimmerit*, made from Tamiya two-part putty, was ridged with two sizes of flat screwdriver heads, the narrower one for the hull and the wider one for the turret.

Upper hull

The main upper hull piece is also very well moulded, complete with accurate turret splash ring, correct overall layout and separate grille and engine hatch panels, as well as exquisite weld seams and intake cap details. The grilles themselves come in two parts and go together to form a very convincing replica of the original. The kit-provided mesh covers were then added; they come pre-formed with the bend on the outer sides, ensuring a snug fit.

I then focused on the tow cable stowage clamps, as well as the numerous tools and tool clamps situated on the hull roof and engine deck. DML offers two options for a complete set of tools, including the often-overlooked starter crank, one with the clamps moulded together with the tools and one clean. I opted for the clean tools and used the etched clamps provided. The Bosch headlight is crisply moulded, with fine detail, and a pre-formed cable wire that fits nicely into the two ready-made holes on the hull roof electrical junction and the headlight base. The kit offers braided wire for modelling the tow cables, along with separate hollowed-out ends, so I used them to make one cable, which I decided to show ready-shackled for immediate use in case of breakdown, attaching it to the shackle via one of the two towing clevises provided. I ran it through the stowage clamps, leaving the other end dangling somewhat dramatically. Again, I annealed the wire before use to make it more pliable. I left off the other cable, indicating its loss through damage.

I used the plastic front right mudguard, thinning the inner edge for a scale look, leaving off the left for visual interest. The real mudguards were hinged to

BELOW, LEFT The internal radiator/fuel cell and cooling fan subassemblies have been painted primer red and fixed in place. The fan blades have been metallized.

BELOW, RIGHT The kit-provided photo-etched sets are quite extensive and provide sufficient parts to detail virtually all the fittings to an acceptable standard.

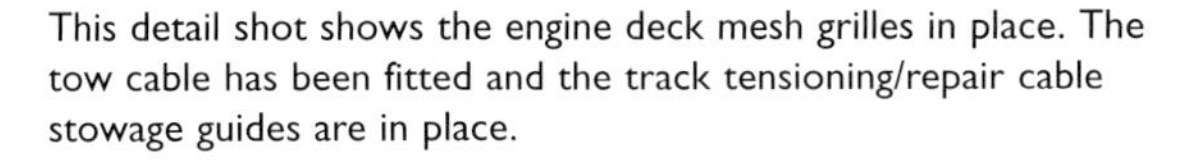

This detail shot shows the engine deck mesh grilles in place. The tow cable has been fitted and the track tensioning/repair cable stowage guides are in place.

The front end of the tow cable and in this view the track tensioning/repair cable is now in place. Note the spare track appliqué on the hull front. At this point the hooks for them have not yet been fitted and neither have the track pins.

The model after the completion of construction. Only several fragile details remain to be fitted after painting and weathering.

allow them to be flipped up for servicing the track, so removing it meant recreating the hinge loops that were welded onto the glacis plate. These were made from thinned styrene tube. The mudguard-retaining hooks and braces are provided as photo-etched components. I used the brace for the right mudguard, but rebuilt the hooks from styrene as the etched ones looked too flat.

I assembled two runs of the white-metal tracks and test-fitted them to the running gear to ascertain how many links were needed. Friulmodel is very generous and I was glad to note that there were plenty of links left over for using as appliqué armour. Three each were attached to either side of the hull front plate, just behind the mudguards, and when their positions had been determined, simple hooks were fashioned out of brass to hold them. Track pins were made using steel wire with plastic discs for the heads.

The turret

DML has moulded the asymmetrical turret as a single piece, with the eight flush roof screws, correctly offset side vision ports and a separate escape hatch with choice of hinges. The 40mm thickened roof plate is offered with two options, with and without the central weld seam. Since mine was to be a May/June vehicle, I opted to go with the simplified roof with the central seam, Pilsen roof crane supports and also the smaller cut-down hinge for the escape hatch, which was so designed to clear the turret splashguard ring. I used the typical late-style mantlet with the reinforced middle and monocular sight and the standard muzzle brake. The basic components went together easily and had *Zimmerit* applied in the same fashion as the hull described earlier.

The turret stowage box provided is acceptable, and hasps are provided for both covers. Later, after priming, I decided that it looked too plain and uninteresting so I shaved down some parts of the side and back and tore holes in it, to simulate shrapnel damage. The exposed edges were scraped paper thin and carefully bent to look as close to sheet metal as possible. Next, the kit anti-aircraft machine-gun mount was improved using fine wire and styrene sheet and rod.

The spare track holders provided lack grab handles, so tiny holes were drilled and fine wires bent to shape added.

Painting

There was so much metal on this tank that I felt it prudent to first coat all the photo-etch and white-metal parts, as well as the tracks, with Gunze metal primer before finally spraying everything with Gunze 1200 general primer.

The kit-provided photo-etched sets are quite extensive and provide sufficient parts to detail virtually all the fittings to an acceptable standard. Here you can also see the hasps for the turret stowage box, and also the hull side skirts, that have been treated to show the effects of wear and battle damage.

The turret, almost completed. The Friulmodel tracks required a track pinhead and locking bolt to be attached to every section. The wire attaching the track run to the trunnion hinge was only a temporary measure and would be replaced later.

Since the large turret stowage box seemed so uninspiring I added some shrapnel damage on it. This was achieved by thinning the surface of the box and then tearing holes in it, to make it look like ripped sheet metal.

A general view of the constructed model with all major components in place. The exhaust shrouds have been tacked in place but will be removed for painting.

This side profile of the constructed model shows the effect of lowering the suspension. The tank does not have that springy, athletic look but rather a more tired, settled one, having pushed its torsion bars to the limit.

The model after receiving its primer coat.

The basic 'tree branch' camouflage pattern in German red-brown has been applied, while the barrel has received a coat of German Grey.

Flaws were corrected and touched up and then the hull, turret and wheels were sprayed with Gunze Dark Yellow (39) lightened with a little Sail (45) and a touch of Khaki (55). I generally spray a 20 per cent lighter-than-normal tone of colour on vehicles with *Zimmerit* as they darken significantly during weathering due to the ridged surfaces. Surfaces not directly facing sunlight were sprayed with straight Gunze Dark Yellow to simulate shadow. The gun barrel of '322' in my reference pictures seemed darker than the rest of the tank, indicating that the barrel might be new. So I sprayed the barrel Panzer Grey, but toned it down with a bit of Dark Yellow and Sail, to create colour sympathy. I noticed that while vehicles of the first and second company of s.Pz.Abt.507 sported a three-tone camouflage, vehicles of the third company tended to have only two, so my camouflage pattern was the fairly typical 'tree-branch' style in a medium red brown, varying in width and intensity from area to area to create a more visually interesting 3D effect. I left the wheels in plain yellow. Once all was dry, I proceeded to paint in the details like tool heads, wooden shafts, machine-gun barrels, periscopes, spare tracks, track pins, etc. The rims of the steel wheels and the sprocket teeth received some 'metallizing' using toned-down silver acrylic paint.

The unit insignia came from Archer dry transfers (AR35136 – Tiger Battalion Insignias). I transferred them onto some decal paper before applying them to the *Zimmerit* surfaces, namely above the driver's visor in the front and on the

The hooks for mounting the front appliqué tracks have now been attached and track pins added. Note the loops for the missing mudguard below the tracks.

The model has now been painted and camouflaged. The camouflage was likely sprayed while all the side skirts were intact, which is why the areas under the missing skirts were left in plain yellow.

Turret numerals were painted in by first airbrushing basic black numbers with a stencil, and then filling in the centres with white paint. The numbers on the left-hand side turret appliqué tracks were painted full size in pure white with no borders. Pictures show the process after the white was added and before final touching up of the borders with black acrylic.

top left corner of the rear plate. Decal softener from Gunze helped them snuggle down for a good fit. The kit *Balkankreuz* decals were applied to either side of the hull.

I made stencils for the rather unique style and size of the numbering system that s.Pz.Abt.507 employed, studying photographs of the real thing beforehand. The company number, for example, was significantly larger than the following numerals. I judged the size in relation to the turret in the photographs and used the same proportions for my stencils. The unit numerals were white with a black outline, so I masked off the relevant areas and, using my homemade stencil, sprayed matt black numerals onto the turret right side and stowage box. On the left-hand side I only sprayed the company number '3' since the spare tracks would cover the rest. Then the white areas of the numbers were filled in using Vallejo acrylics, touching up with some black wherever necessary. The right-hand side numbers were hand painted on the spare track in white only, but positioned so as to be in line with the existing company number painted earlier on the turret.

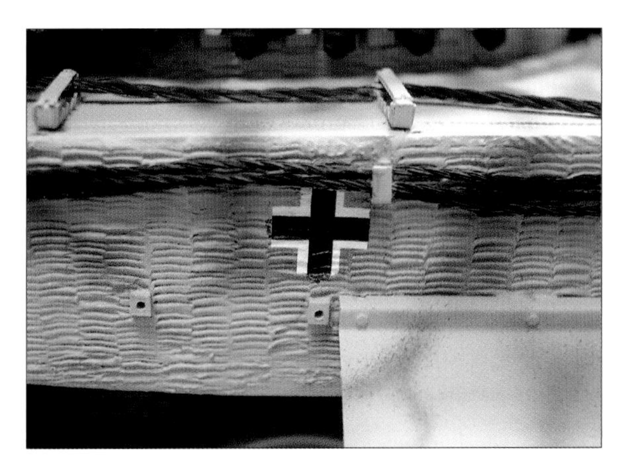

Balkan cross decals were applied straight onto the *Zimmerit* and helped to settle down snugly with Gunze's decal setting solution.

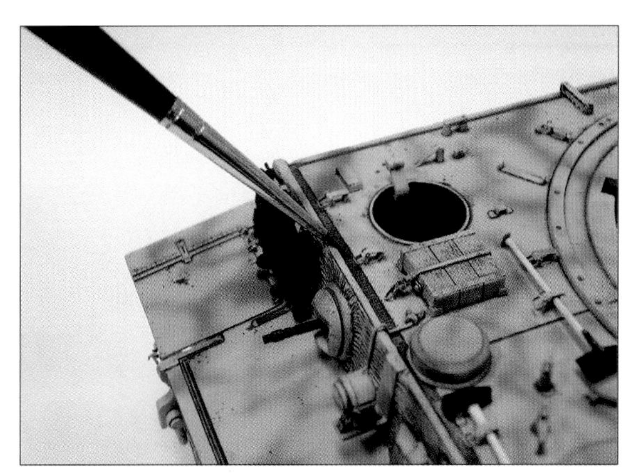

Thinned Vallejo acrylics were carefully painted into the deepest grooves to suggest very dark shadows and accentuate contrast. Water run-off streaks were simulated using even thinner mixtures of Vallejo acrylics in shades of grey and brown. Subtlety is the key.

Weathering and finishing touches

Abrasions and scratches from crew passage, shrapnel and other such abuse were simulated using Vallejo acrylics (822 SS Camouflage Black Brown and 872 Chocolate). These I carefully and subtly added, trying to avoid creating large unrealistic patches. The overall idea was to give an idea of controlled intensity. Deep shadows and panel lines were accentuated by painting them using a 000 brush, working in thin layers rather than one thick application. Subtle streaks and water run-off marks were also created using varying shades of grey and brown with high dilution (10:1). Specific details around the upper hull were also highlighted using a lighter but compatible tone of the basecoat yellow mixed with Vallejo acrylics.

Next, I primed the model for washes by first brushing on distilled turpentine, then adding lightly tinted washes of various hues to accentuate tonal variety on the rather plain-looking camouflage. Next I applied a pin wash with a heavier consistency to bring out darker shadows, panel lines and so forth using Winsor & Newton oils (Raw Umber, Black, Golden Ochre and Burnt Umber). I finished off by spraying the exhaust shroud interiors and nearby engine deck in a sooty black-brown colour. The shrouds were then glued on permanently, ready for further weathering.

To depict the effects of the muddy terrain so often encountered on the Eastern Front by the Panzerwaffe, I prepared a mud mixture by mixing some fine brick dust with Tamiya polyester putty and some thinner, which was coloured dirty brown with a mixture of Dark Earth, Black, Dark Yellow and Khaki Tamiya acrylics. The resultant sludge was then carefully applied to the undersides, especially to areas where an accumulation of mud and dirt would be expected.

The tracks were painted a dirty dark-brown colour and then ground pastel powder of varying earthy tones mixed with Tamiya acrylic thinner was brushed on. When dry, other tones were randomly applied, and this process continued until a convincing look was achieved. These same tones were then applied to the lower hull areas for consistency. Dry pastel powders of similar tones were then dusted on to make a smooth transition between upper and lower hulls while maintaining an overall colour sympathy that would look nice but still be realistic. Raised edges of the tracks were scraped to simulate wear and abrasion during use, allowing the bare metal to show through in specific areas. Once complete the tracks were carefully fitted and a final dusting of chalks was applied.

Finally, the pre-painted wing nuts and fragile detail parts were added and, through pin washes and detailed highlighting, were integrated into the completed model.

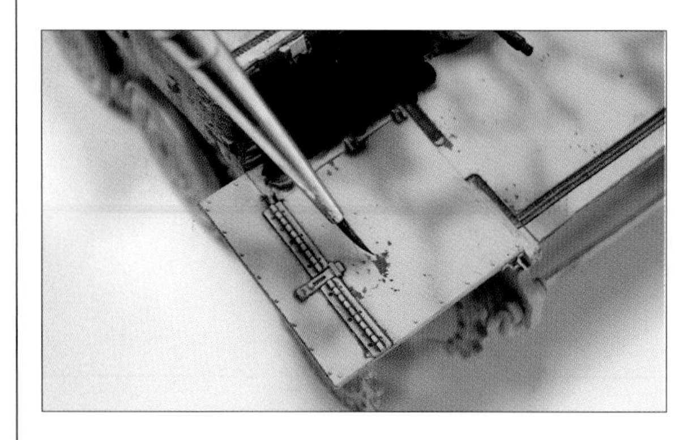

Detail shots showing the process of painting in chips and abrasions and outlining hard edges to shadows or panel lines.

Light filters and washes were applied using thinned oil paints to both soften the somewhat stark contrast between shadows and highlights and also create tonal variations of the base colours.

LEFT and MIDDLE Two photographs showing the wash process, including primer wash and tinting, to accentuate the Zimmerit pattern and darker washes to accentuate dirt and shadows and panel lines. Care was taken to ensure that smudges and spills were cleaned up so that details remained tight.

Unless my vehicle is to become part of a diorama, I usually avoid muddying up the wheels and tracks too much, as such application has no context and hides a lot of detail. Conversely, a model with clean wheels and tracks in a muddy diorama environment would look out of place too.

A gentle overspray of the mud colour applied to the substructure helps create a smooth transition from the lower to the upper hull.

The insides and tops of the exhaust shrouds and stacks were sprayed a dirty brownish black, replicating the sooty deposits produced by the exhaust gases.

Various parts were highlighted including edges and raised detail using a colour compatible with the basecoat prepared with Vallejo acrylic paint.

Two shots showing the overall appearance of the finished vehicle.

Detail shots of the front of the finished vehicle. Note the unit insignia above the driver's armoured visor.

Detail close-up of the loader's hatch showing the level of detail incorporated in the DML kit as well as the lanyard made from fine wire.

Detail shot of the left rear. Again, the unit insignia is clearly visible.

'1331', 13./SS-Panzer Regiment 1, Kursk 1943 (1/35 scale)

Subject:	*Tiger I '1331', 13./SS-Panzer Regiment 1, Kursk, July 1943 (Early Production, April/May 1943)*
Modeller:	*Gary Edmundson*
Skill level:	*Intermediate*
Base kit:	*Cyber-Hobby Tiger I Initial Production DAK (6286); Dragon Models Ltd Tiger I Late Production (6253) Tamiya Tiger I Frühe Production (TM35216)*
Scale:	*1/35*
Additional detailing sets used:	*WWII Productions Early Tiger Track Links (35027), Royal Model Detail set (158)*

Introduction

On 5 July 1943, 12 Tiger I tanks belonging to 13./SS-Panzer Regiment 1 began their first attack of the battle of Kursk. Lasting 11 days, it was the biggest tank battle of World War II. The Tiger I commanded by Michael Wittmann during the battle had the tactical number '1331'. No known photos presently exist of this vehicle. Pictures of '1332' and '1334' have shown them to be later variants of the early-production Tiger, and photos of '1311' and '1313' show them to be of the previously manufactured type. It was assumed for this project that Wittmann's '1331' would have been the later type, built between mid-April and mid-May 1943.

Cyber-Hobby's DAK Tiger I was used as a base kit to make an early-production Tiger used by Michael Wittmann during the Kursk battles in July 1943.

The Cyber-Hobby DAK Tiger kit was used as a basis for the model, utilizing additional parts from the DML late Tiger I, and Tamiya's early-production Tiger I. Reference used was the Jentz and Doyle book *Germany's Tiger Tanks D.W. to Tiger I – Design, Development and Modifications* (Schiffer Publishing, 2000), which has drawings of a May 1943 production vehicle.

Running gear

The rubber-tyred roadwheels and lower hull from the DAK Tiger kit were used for the model. The hull has the two small access hatches on the bottom indicative of the earlier Maybach HL 210 P 45 engine that this vehicle had. MIG Productions' resin detail set for the initial-production DML Tiger I includes roadwheels that have lost their rubber. Two of these wheels were used on the left side of the vehicle with a missing wheel to simulate battle or mine damage. The plastic on two of the wheels was thinned from the rear and punctured with a sharp hobby blade simulating holes from shrapnel hits. Although the kit allows 'workable' torsion bar suspension, the swing arms for the roadwheels were glued solid to ease the addition of the track links and final sit of the model. The drive sprockets were modified from the DAK Tiger by flattening the hub with a Dremel tool, and adding the bolt pattern cut from the late-pattern sprockets. The rear idler mounting post was squeezed with a pair of pliers for a very tight friction fit that allowed positioning to take place after the tracks were added.

The kit's track links were replaced with World War II Productions' resin 'click' links that have the early pattern tread and holes for the guide teeth.

The track cable was positioned according to reference in the book Germany's *Tiger Tanks D.W. to Tiger I: Design, Production and Modifications* by Thomas L. Jentz and Hilary L. Doyle. Styrene strip and Modelkasten wing nuts helped complete the details.

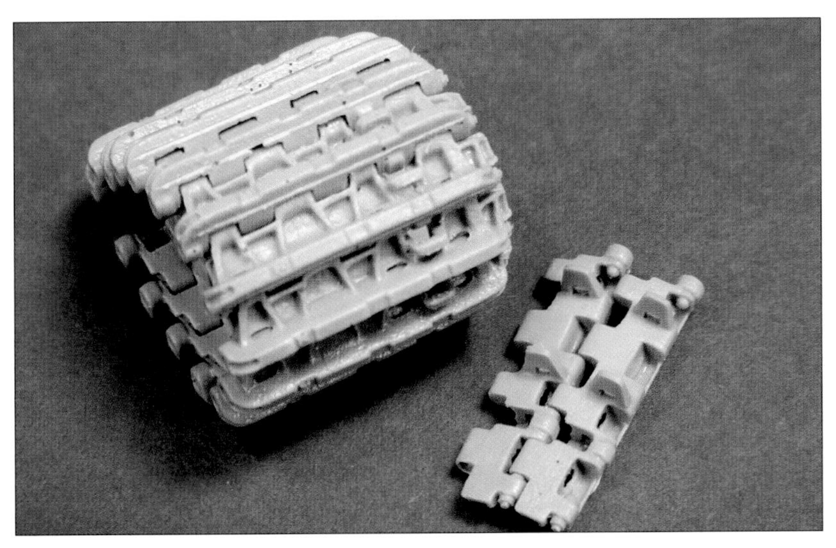

WWII Productions' resin track links were added to the running gear. These were the earlier type with no cleat pattern on the face. The links were cleaned with an appropriately sized drill bit, and then pressed together.

Shrapnel damage was added to the running gear by thinning the plastic from behind and forming jagged holes with a hobby blade. The roadwheels missing the rubber tyre were from a detail set from MIG Productions.

Hull construction

The front towing pintles were rebuilt using .060in.-thick styrene, tracing the outline from the drawing in Jentz and Doyle's *D.W. to Tiger I* book. The front plate in front of the driver was replaced with MIG Productions' battle-damaged resin part that features detail of anti-tank hits. The plate was too narrow to fit the hull width exactly, and epoxy putty was used to give it the required dimension, with weld marks being scratched into each side. The driver's binocular holes in the front plate were filled with putty.

The late-production engine deck was mated to the DAK Tiger upper hull plate. The left-hand glycol filler port was made to match the right-hand side that had a rectangular-shaped base. Later-pattern rear engine deck grilles were used. The latch for the engine deck hatch was moved to line up with its anchor, and the Feifel air hose right-hand side bracket was moved to accommodate this relocation. The hatch handles (J14) and stops (C6, 7, 10) were added to the engine access hatch, although they're not mentioned in the DAK Tiger instructions. The rear hatch in the centre of the deck featured a triangular plate that indicated the later Maybach HL 230 P45, but this hatch design was introduced on the vehicles before the newer engines were installed, and therefore would have been installed on Wittmann's vehicle.

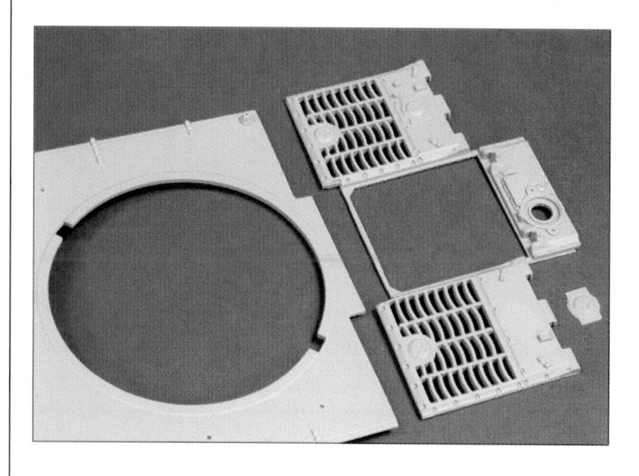

The upper hull of the DAK Tiger was mated to the engine deck of the late-production Tiger, with the coolant filler on the left-hand side made to match the right.

MIG Productions makes a resin replacement for the front upper plate that features realistic battle damage. Since it was slightly narrower than the hull, the edges had to be widened with putty.

The DAK Tiger roof was adapted to DML's late-production turret shell. Tamiya's escape hatch featured the scalloped edges, and replaced the later-style DML part.

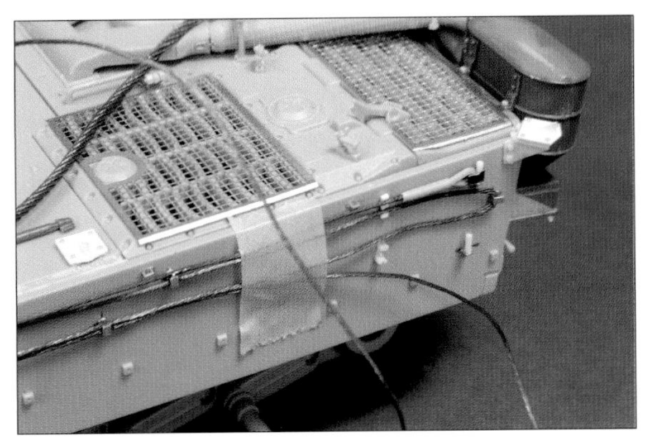

Cable from an old drafting table was used for the kit's equipment. It was attached to the side of the model with Royal Model's etched-metal and resin brackets. The Tamiya tape was a great help for holding things in place while the glue dried.

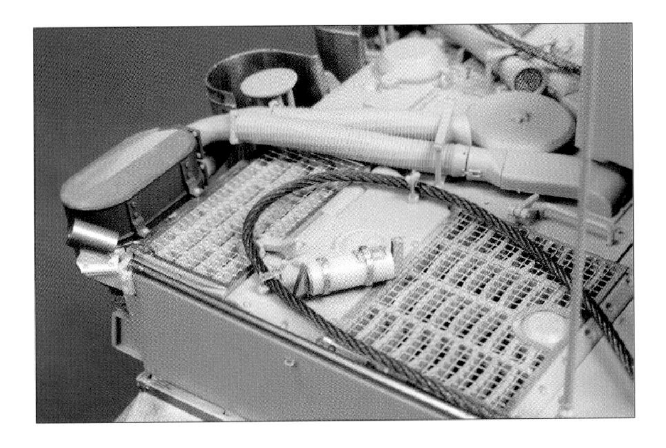

Tamiya's later-style Feifel air filters were added to the model and the flange connections for the hoses were detailed with hexagonal bolts on both sides. The 'S' mine launchers on the hull were made from the brass DAK Tiger smoke candle launchers intended for the turret. The vehicles from 13./SS-Panzer Regiment 1 had their turret-mounted smoke candles removed.

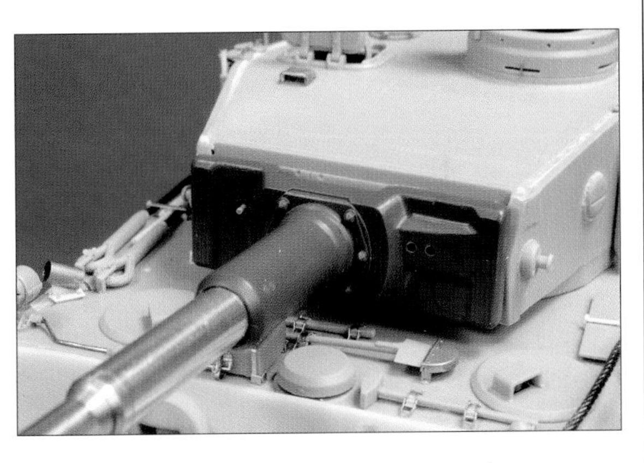

The mantlet from Tamiya's Frühe Tiger I fitted the DML base parts well, and best represented the type on an April/May 1943-production vehicle. Small screw heads were added to the sleeve using a flat syringe needle to make the circular impression, followed by a jeweller's screwdriver to make the slot.

Brass exhaust shrouds from DML's Tiger Late Production kit were mounted on styrene blocks on the rear plate. The toolbox from the Tamiya kit was modified with styrene and brass details, and mounted on a support from Royal Model.

Brass fenders on the side and front were from the DML late-production kit. The lower edge of the side fenders had a strip of styrene added since the folded lip is missing from the kit part.

The model's tow cables had a fair amount of spring in them, and therefore had to be anchored with brass pins at the points of the cable brackets.

'S' mine (*Schrapnellmine*) dischargers were constructed and mounted on the hull in five locations using the DAK Tiger brass parts mounted on styrene bases. The notches on the edge were moved to the rear, and filled with putty where a styrene strip had been added. The electrical ignition wire was made from thin solder, glued into a hole on the end and fed down into the hull. The ones on the rear corners of the hull hang over the edge, and were glued onto resin mounts from the Royal Model detail set.

The watertight cover for air inlet was stowed on the hull's left-hand side just behind the driver's hatch with a styrene bracket. The kit's towing cables were replaced with more realistic-looking cable salvaged from an old drafting table arm. Finer material was used for the track cable, and was fastened to the hull's left-hand side with Royal Model details and some styrene parts. The locations of the DAK gun-cleaning rod mounts were removed from the upper hull and replacements from the Royal Model set were added.

DML's brass side fenders were added to the model, with a thin strip of styrene glued under the lower edge to add the fold that is missing. The fender section above the missing wheel on the left-hand side was left off and the adjacent fender bent to simulate recent damage. A brass front mudflap from the DML late kit was soldered together and glued onto the right side of the vehicle using the plastic hinge detail, which was sliced from sprue part F5.

Rear plate

Mounted vertically between the two exhaust pipes, the starter assist plate was the type indicating that the vehicle had the earlier engine. The standard exhaust armoured covers and brass shields from the late kit were used (not the specialized DAK ones).

The later-style toolbox from the Tamiya kit was spruced up with some etched-metal and styrene detail and mounted above the left-hand mudflap. The rear mudflaps on the vehicle still may have had the welded mounting frames, which were discontinued around May 1943. This was discovered after

The fenders had the strengthening ribs soldered in place underneath. To show the result of an explosion, one of the sections was pre-bent with a pair of pliers before installation.

the model had been completed. Tamiya's later Feifel air-cleaner canisters were added to the model with very fine etched-metal retaining chains glued to the rear plugs. Bolt detail was placed on all sides of the Feifel air-cleaner flanges where it was missing. The bolts were obtained by shaving them from the underside of a surplus DML Panzer IV hull. The plastic Feifel hoses from the DAK Tiger I have the correct 12-sided corrugated circumference, as opposed to the braided tubing that was supplied in the kit as an alternative part.

Turret

To construct an early-pattern Tiger turret, parts from all three base kits were combined. The late Tiger turret housing was used with Tamiya's escape hatch that features the bevelled edges. The turret side vision slots were replaced with ones from the DAK turret, which have the slot correctly positioned slightly lower than the mid point. Two troughs in the lower edges on each side of the turret chin had to be filled with putty. Tamiya's mantlet was combined with DML's mounting parts since it has the correct reinforced part on the left-hand side by the binocular sight. Photos of tanks from 13./SS-Panzer Regiment 1 around the time of the Kursk battles showed the turret-mounted smoke dischargers had been removed.

A loader's periscope was added to the DAK Tiger turret roof, and a 3.25mm x 5.25mm x 1.8mm armoured cover was made out of thick lead sheet from a tube of ski wax. Wing nuts were added to the vent cover on the turret roof, although most crews left this waterproofing cover off. The later stowage bin was mounted on the turret rear. The left-hand side turret spare track mounts were moved closer together and forward, since they are too close to the rear turret pistol port. Three spare track links were added to the left-hand side of the turret, since the vehicle could possibly be one of approximately 25 that were so equipped with this early configuration. A photo in Wolfgang Schneider's *Tigers In Combat II* (J.J. Fedorowicz Publishing, 1998) of a Tiger I on a railcar said to have been for this SS-Panzer Regiment, dated 13 May 1943, shows this spare

To add to the beaten appearance, the front left mudguard was left off. Hinge detail was shaved from the optional DML glacis part with a pair of pliers and added to the model.

The two crew figures were resin figurines from Alpine miniatures. Show Modelling's Wittmann figure provided the head for the commander.

track arrangement. Pins were added to the spare tracks using .025in. rod that was heated and slightly melted to flatten the top ends.

Painting

After priming the model with a dark-brown Floquil lacquer, it was basecoated in a Tamiya acrylic mixture of *Dunkelgelb*. Camouflage stripes of thinned Tamiya Olive Green followed, after which the details were all painted with Vallejo watercolours. The tyres on the roadwheels were painted with Floquil's Weathered Black. Decals were applied to the turret from various sources to get the correct size and shape of the numbers. The centres of the numbers were painted with dark yellow by mixing some Vallejo watercolours to get the matching shade.

To give a rich tone to the overall colour of the model, SIN Industries' Filter P241 was brushed onto the painted surface. This had to be well stirred and carefully applied, since it tended to settle quickly and darken some areas more than others. While the surface was still damp, thinned raw umber oil paint was added to enhance some of the model's fine details.

A crew was added using Alpine Miniatures figurines. The commander figure representing Michael Wittmann received a well-sculpted head from the Show Modelling figure of the same name. The figures' uniforms were finished in a spring oakleaf pattern following Calvin Tan's method outlined in the Osprey Modelling 23: *Modelling Waffen SS Figures* (Oxford, 2006).

The model was given a camouflage scheme of dark yellow with olive-green stripes using Tamiya's acrylic paints. The missing fender section was masked off since the area would have been free from the green spray.

Various decals were used to piece together the turret numbers '1331' to obtain the appropriate size and style. The earlier vehicles in 13./SS-Panzer Regiment 1 without spare tracks on the turret had larger numbers.

Once in place, the turret numbers were painted with Vallejo watercolour paints, which have a very solid pigment and apply very smoothly.

To weather the model, it was treated to an application of a filter from SIN Industries. This mineral-spirit-based wash enriched the colour of the model, and allowed the surface to be dampened for the addition of darker oil paint. Raw umber was thinned with mineral spirits and added to some of the smaller details.

To paint the tracks, they were first airbrushed with a dirt colour using a mix of Floquil lacquer paints. Several different colours of chalk pastels were ground on sandpaper and placed into small aluminium dishes.

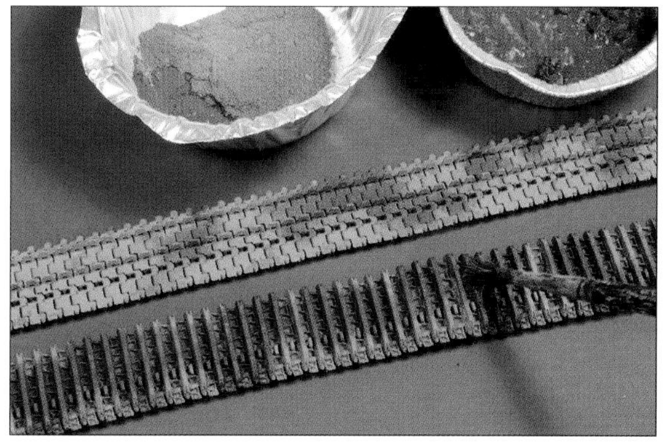

The pastel dust was mixed with Tamiya's acrylic thinner and daubed onto the track runs randomly. This was done on both sides of the track, and the colours were alternated and made to look patchy.

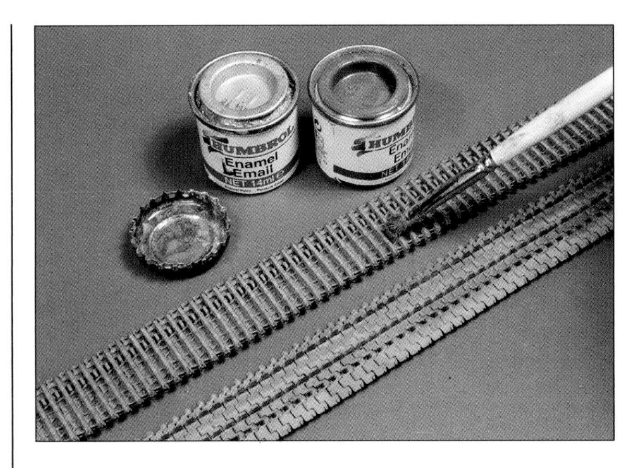

When dry, the track runs were heavily drybrushed using an old stubby paintbrush with Humbrol Silver and Steel enamels. The pastels tend to tone down the look of the metallic paint.

The high points of the track links and edges of the damaged roadwheel were rubbed with Humbrol's Silver and Steel enamels.

After painting the model with its initial scheme and with all details painted and decals applied, it was given an overall spray with dirt-coloured Tamiya acrylics, thinned to five per cent paint.

Pastel chalks were used to weather the rear of the vehicle and the running gear.

Thinned oil paint was placed randomly on some of the details, and dragged in a downward direction to simulate rain marks.

A vignette was made using a trophy plaque as a base, and groundwork formed with Aves Master Mache. Heki's tall grass comes in the form of a mat that was teased apart and glued into place.

Two infantry figures were converted from various Dragon figure sets to depict the early-style Waffen-SS camouflage uniforms in service during the summer of 1943.

'F05', Gruppe Fehrmann, Germany 1945 (1/35 scale)

Subject:	*Tiger I 'F05', Gruppe Fehrmann, April 1945*
Modeller:	*Darren Thompson*
Skill level:	*Intermediate*
Base kit:	*Dragon Models Ltd Tiger I Initial Production (6252); Dragon Models Ltd Tiger I Late Production (6253); Cyber-Hobby Tiger I Initial Production DAK (6286)*
Scale:	*1/35*
Additional detailing sets used:	*Aber Tiger I Early (35014); Aber Tiger I Late (35015); Aber Tiger I Early Barrel (35L26); Friulmodel Tiger I Mid/Late Tracks (ATL-06); Artisan Mori German 20t Jack (MGP-15); Schatton-Modellbau German Antenna (3524); Karaya TC Tow Cables*

A brief history

In early April, 1945, the sole remaining Tiger I of Gruppe Fehrmann still in operation found itself behind enemy lines and on the retreat. 'F05', now under the command of Major Paul Schulze, had already been in several heavy firefights with both British and American troops since leaving Fallingbostel and it now ran into another engagement with the US 5th Armored Division. Despite sustaining three hits, 'F05' managed to knock out three M4 Shermans and an armoured car before escaping. By chance, Schulze came across a

'F05' completed.

US tanker truck and was able to re-fuel before making a break for the German lines. Another enemy engagement followed and more US vehicles were destroyed, resulting in a number of Americans surrendering to Schulze and the handing over of 200 German POWs. After continuing its escape, 'F05' finally ran out of fuel and had to be blown up by its own crew.

The model

As there are no known photographs of 'F05', the features I wished to create were based on the other vehicles from that group, which also allowed me a degree of artistic licence. I decided to follow similar build features to 'F01', an early Tiger that had been refitted with late features, including *Zimmerit* on the hull, steel wheels and late-pattern tracks. Also, to suggest later repairs, I decided to use an early turret, retro-fitted from another vehicle, with late-style track hangers and a different camouflage scheme. As a model, there is no way to build this vehicle out of the box, so I chose to combine both the initial Tiger I and the late Tiger I, from DML.

The lower hull

For the lower hull, I combined the early tub with the late suspension arms and late hull sides, as these provided the side-skirt mounts moulded in place. The only alterations necessary to the lower hull were to the front glacis plate. The front mudguard mounts were added, along with a fillet along the bottom front edge of the sponsons. The outer joints of the front glacis were also remodelled, to turn the initial type into an early. The upper hull was created by cutting the initial engine grilles away and replacing them with the engine grilles from the late hull, as these provide the correct water filler hatches. Once the main elements of the hull were assembled and the glue cured, it was time to add the *Zimmerit* coating, before any of the smaller details.

The upper hull

Once the *Zimmerit* had fully cured, the remnants of the smoke grenade launchers and Feifel air cleaners were added. These were made from a combination of plastic strip and elements of the Aber early Tiger detail set, with the exception of the forked housing, which came from the Cyber-Hobby DAK Tiger I.

All the tool location holes were filled, using stretched sprue and liquid cement, and Aber tool stowage was added, re-positioned to suit an early Tiger I. I decided to leave most of the tool holders empty, to add to the vehicle's battle-weary look.

The brass exhaust housings and the side skirts were both supplied as pre-formed items in the DML Late kit and were suitably damaged with small pliers. To finish the rear hull, the engine starter attachment was converted to represent the early type, then mounted into the starter housing rather than its stowage mount.

The turret

As with the hull, both initial and late kits were combined to give the required features. The late turret shell was used, as the initial shell doesn't provide for a turret escape hatch; however, the hatch cover itself does need its side edges bevelled and the hinge rebate filled. It was then a simple case of adding the left-hand pistol port to the turret rear. To fit the initial roof it was necessary to remove a small amount of material from the roof edge, as the late turret walls are slightly thicker.

Part of the late refit would have included removing the turret smoke launchers, reproduced with plastic strip and Milliput welds. The turret-mounted track holders were also fitted from the late kit, and the commander's hatch support was cut down to enable the hatch to lie horizontally, a fairly common field modification.

Zimmerit

My material of choice, for *Zimmerit*, is Milliput Superfine White. This two-part putty is kneaded together, in equal parts, until thoroughly mixed. Leaving it for a few minutes, to allow the stickiness to lessen slightly, gives just enough time to prepare the surfaces of the model, to which the finish is being applied.

A Scotchbrite pad is used in a circular motion to 'key' the surface and give the Milliput something to bite into. I apply the Milliput straight onto the model, forcing the putty onto the surface with my thumb, whilst using a slow dragging motion. Any high points that remain are carefully removed with a blade, and then worked over again with my thumb. The intention is not to have a perfectly smooth finish, as a degree of movement in the surface looks far more realistic. Once the areas have a thin, uniform coverage, the Milliput must be left to harden slightly before continuing.

To test the putty for the next stage, I gently push my *Zimmerit* tool into the surface to start the ridging. If the putty stays bonded to the surface and the tool comes away cleanly, try a few more ridges. If the putty starts to come away, or leaves any residue on the tool, leave it a little longer.

Once it is ready, gently press the ridging tool into the putty, in a steady, uniform fashion. I always start from the top and work downwards, holding the tool at a slight downward angle to the surface. Don't worry about any putty build-up between the rows, or any excess putty around the surface details: this can easily be removed later and, to some degree, was a feature of the real thing too. Once the surfaces are covered, I leave the putty to cure further, until quite firm. If you wish to inflict any damage, now is the time. I used two methods on the Tiger: firstly, I used a pointed scalpel blade to cut squarely along some of the ridges and joins, then removed the putty within, by scraping it away; this suggests large chunks that have been knocked off, by either collision, or heavy impacts. Secondly, by simply digging the blade into the surface and flicking the point out to one side, you can recreate damage from small-arms fire. It is also possible to use this method after the model has been painted, as it allows the white *Zimmerit* to show through.

ABOVE, LEFT The start of the *Zimmerit* process. The Milliput is drawn across the surface, while applying downward pressure.

ABOVE, RIGHT The ridges are then recreated with a small screwdriver blade.

LEFT The finished *Zimmerit* complete with battle damage.

A rear view of the Tiger showing the damaged exhaust shrouds.

The engine deck: notice the final remnants of the Feifel air filters.

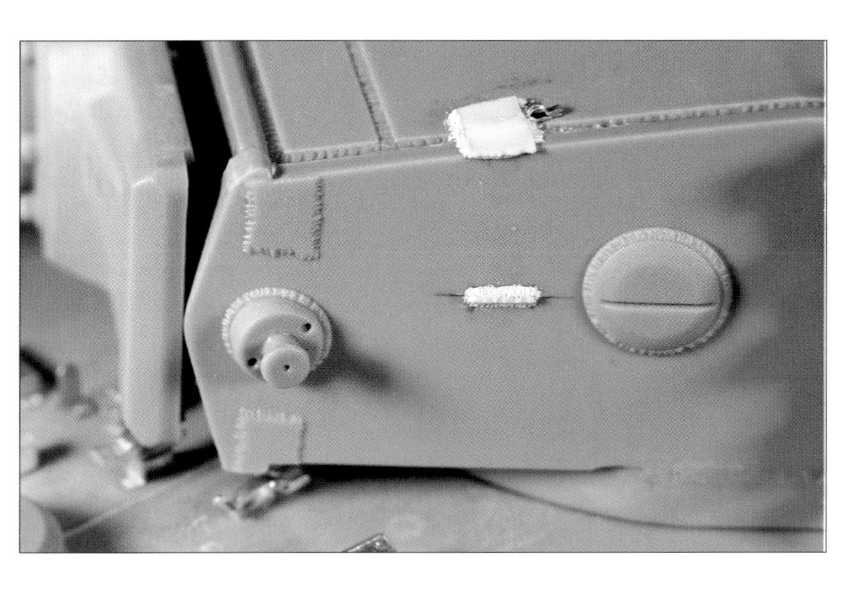

The smoke launchers have been removed; the torch-cut edges are faithfully reproduced here.

The commander's cupola: brass wire has been used to replicate the handle and hatch spring.

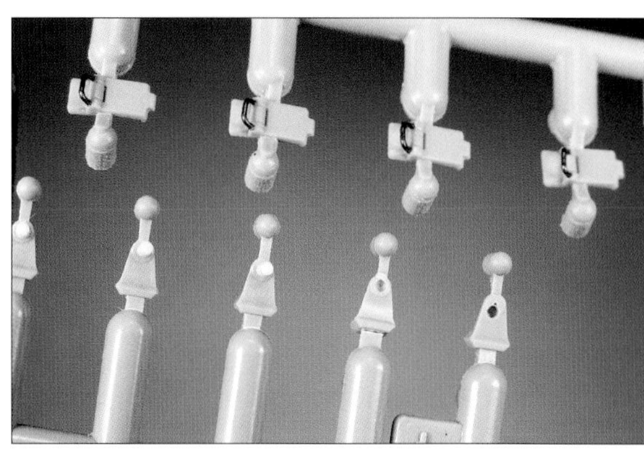

Smaller parts are often easier to work on if left on the sprue.

Construction completed. This view gives a good idea of the different materials used.

The new turret bin in place.

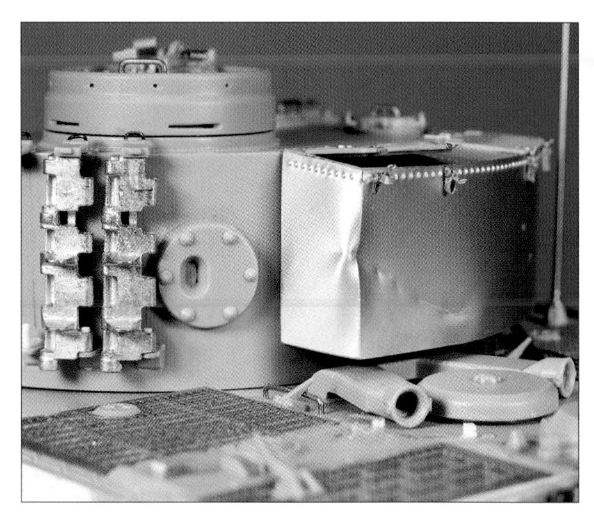

Rear three-quarter view: the superb antenna is from Schatton-Modellbau.

Another feature that I particularly wanted to portray was a damaged turret bin, as two of the known examples are photographed with theirs completely missing. I started by placing a piece of masking tape around the kit part and running a pencil along its edges. This gave me an accurate template, which I could then transfer to some aluminium sheet. The template was cut out and the fold lines scored, with a new blade. I then used a marking-out gauge to reproduce the line of rivets, found along the bin's top edge. By pressing a compass point through the holes in the gauge, into the back of the aluminium, the rivets were formed on the outside of the bin. It was then just a case of replacing the rear portion of the kit bin, with the new piece. The damage was created by gentle pressure from a scalpel handle.

Making a template of the rear turret bin.

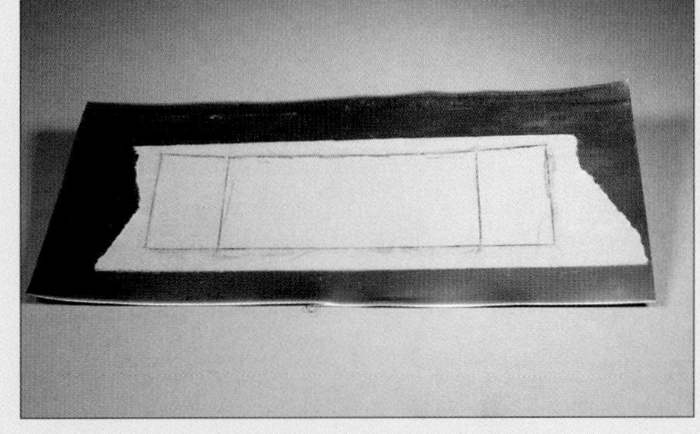

The template in place on the aluminium sheet.

The new part now has the rivet detail in place, punched from the wrong side.

Rolling the centre portion of the bin. The part is placed on a piece of soft rubber. The more pressure that is applied, the tighter the radius, so start gently and check often!

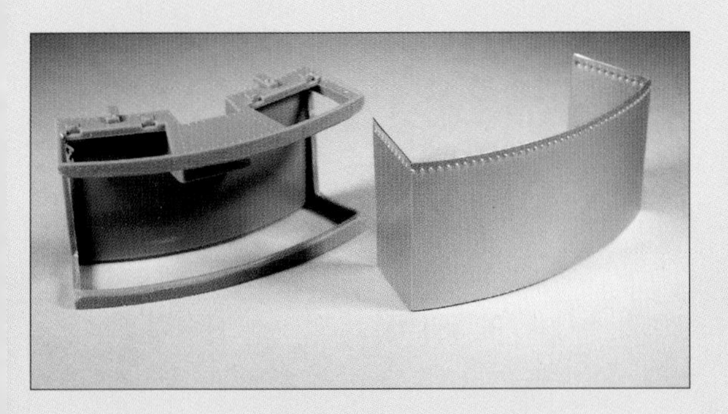

The new part waiting to be fitted.

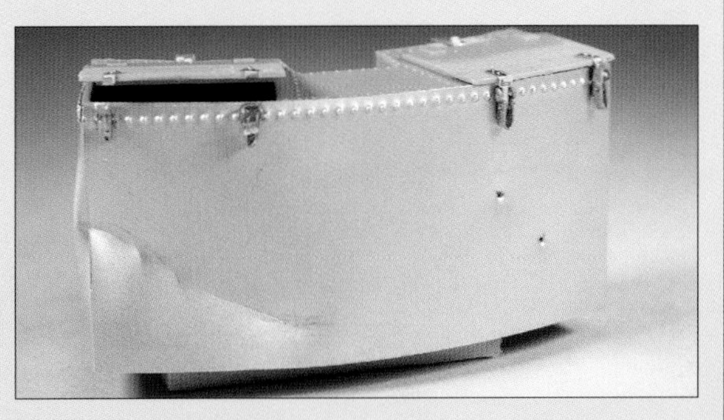

The finished bin, complete with bullet holes.

Painting and weathering

After applying my usual aerosol primer, all parts were given a basecoat of Tamiya Dark Yellow (XF-60). The turret and some of the wheels were then given a second coat, with about 20 per cent white added, to start giving the effect that the tank had been made up from parts of several vehicles. To further strengthen this idea, some of the wheels were painted with red primer, White Ensign enamel 'RN WWII anti-fouling', and the turret bin was painted with the original Panzer Grey, again from White Ensign. The barrel was also given a coat of very dark grey, which was a common shade seen on newly fitted barrels yet to be painted. This was mixed from Tamiya German Grey and Black. The camouflage was airbrushed free hand, using broad red-brown patches for the turret and the more common three-tone scheme on the hull.

The markings were hand-painted onto the turret sides and rear bin, by firstly cutting a masking tape stencil. This was airbrushed, with the same red primer as before, followed by a thin, brush-painted border, in an off-white.

A coat of Tamiya Gloss was applied next to enable the following filters to distribute evenly. These filters were mixed from raw umber and raw sienna oils and a large amount of Humbrol thinners, the idea being that subtle variations in tone can be produced, by varying the colour mix and the amount of layers applied between the different areas of the tank. This was then followed by various pin washes, again using the same oils, to accentuate the raised detail. Once thoroughly dry, the glossy finish was knocked back, with a couple of coats of Vallejo Matt Varnish.

The basic colours laid down: notice the camouflage is masked from where the skirts would have been.

The turret has received a gloss coat and some filters. Notice how the colours have darkened already.

The first oil wash has been applied to the *Zimmerit*. The original *Dunkelgrau* is showing through where the *Zimmerit* has been lost.

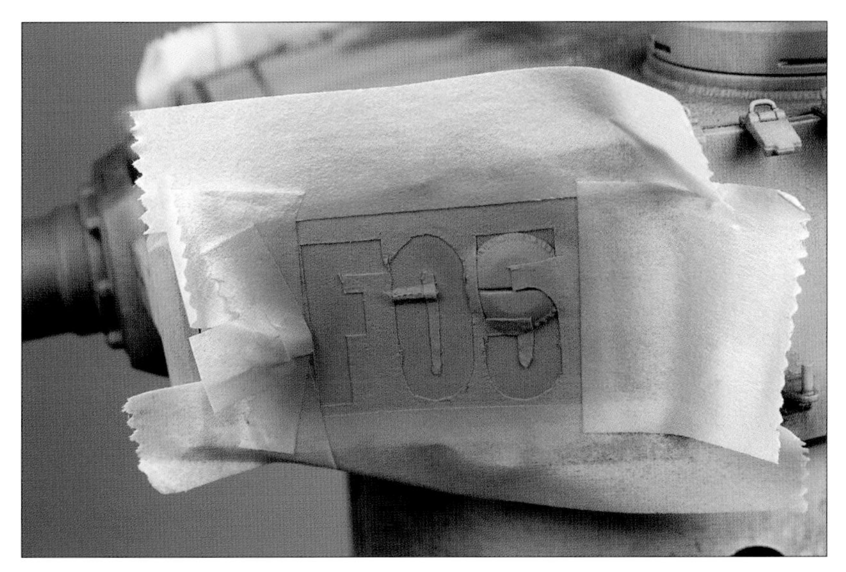

'F05', drawn freehand on Tamiya tape. Red primer was used for the base colour.

Small chips were sponged on with a piece of dense foam. Larger scratches were added with a fine brush.

Notice how the application of the pigments has calmed the brightness of the chips, giving them a far more realistic look.

Weathering the roadwheels, clockwise from the top. 1. Basecoat only. 2. Gloss coat and oil wash. 3. Lightened base colour is used to 'clean' the high points. 4. Red primer and metallic chips. 5. A pigment wash and a leaky hub. The leak is reproduced with oil paints and gloss varnish.

The next stage was to create the scratching and chipping, again making a marked difference between the hull and the turret. I began by using the sponging technique to create all the fine chip, around the hatches and crew-boarding points, followed by some fine brush-painted scratches using lightened versions of the base colours.

The lower areas of the hull and the wheels were all treated to a light overspray of Humbrol Khaki (72) to begin the dusty finish I was after; this was then further enhanced, by several applications of earth-toned pastels and pigments. The area to be treated was first saturated, with Tamiya thinners, and then the pigments were dropped into the liquid from a brush.

The tracks received a basecoat of Vallejo acrylics German Camo Black Brown (822) and, once dry, the inner running surfaces were marked in using a soft graphite pencil. The same mix of pigments was applied next, only this time mixed into a slurry with Tamiya thinners. The excess was removed from the inner and outer running surfaces when dry. Finally, I gently passed some fine abrasive paper over the outer cleats, to remove the paint and give them a polished finish.

The same earth-toned pigments were used on the rest of the vehicle, firstly as thin washes, then later in their dry form. The washes were applied with downward strokes on all vertical surfaces and with a tapping motion on the

A pigment slurry was brushed onto the tracks. Once dry, most of it was removed with a stiff brush, leaving it only in the recesses.

Subtle highlights have been added to the top edge of the large rust patches to represent flaking paint.

The damaged turret bin finished. Several layers are visible, first, the removed dust, then the edge of the red primer and, finally, the dark metal which is yet to rust, suggesting a recent incident.

The finished running gear. This part of the model is often overlooked, but really deserves as much attention as the rest of the vehicle.

horizontal ones. By mixing the density of the washes different effects can be produced. This can be enhanced further by moving the pigments around with a brush, once they have dried.

At this point just the final touches remained. Fuel spills were reproduced with lightly thinned oil paints, applied in layers and allowed to dry then finished off with a touch of gloss varnish. A selection of the tools, missing from the stowed positions, were painted and assembled on the engine deck.

The advantages of the Friulmodel tracks are perfectly illustrated here. The realistic sag, due to the weight of the individual links, and the highly polished cleats reproduced by removing the paint with some fine abrasive paper.

The completed model. Despite having different colour schemes on the turret and hull, the two were broght together in the weathering process.

'323', Pz.Abt.502, Russia 1943 (1/16 scale)

Subject:	*Tiger I '323', Pz.Abt.502, Russia 1943*
Modeller:	*David Parker*
Skill level:	*Advanced*
Base kit:	*Tamiya 1:16th Early Production Display Model (36203)*
Scale:	*1/16*
Additional detailing sets used:	*Aber Exclusive Edition Upgrade (16K01), S&T Products Tiger 1 Early Tracks (STP-16005)*

Tamiya first released their big 1/16-scale Tiger I back in 2000 with full radio control, including sound effects and recoil action, and it caused quite a stir. Although the kit was designed for radio control I could already see the modelling possibilities, and not long after this Tamiya released a static version of the kit that dispensed with the radio-control equipment but still kept a basic gearbox to allow the kit to be powered. This kit also included an alternative Afrika Korps crew figure and was moulded in a more user-friendly sand plastic instead of the dark grey of the original. Not long after the release of this second version Polish photo-etch maestros Aber released a full detail set to improve the Tamiya kits. Costing almost as much as the base Tamiya kit this comprehensive set includes everything needed to detail and correct the Tamiya kit, including new steel tow cables, solid brass track brackets and no fewer than 19 different etched frets. The combination of the Tamiya kit and the Aber detail set makes for a stark contrast; whilst the Tamiya kit is simple to assemble the Aber detail set is extremely demanding and massively time consuming, but the results make it well worth all the effort.

The subject

The version of the Tiger replicated by Tamiya means my choice of vehicles was immediately restricted. Their kit depicts an early-production vehicle with drum cupola and rubber-rimmed roadwheels. The turret roof periscope mounting is

The finished model photographed from the same angle as the real vehicle that the model was based on depicted complete with the muddy finish shown in that photograph.

missing as are the spare track brackets around the turret; however, the Aber set includes these and I was keen to use them. The kit also has Feifel air filters but the hoses for them are inaccurate so I looked for a vehicle with them removed. After much deliberation I narrowed my choice down to a vehicle serving with Pz.Abt.502 in Russia. Most of their vehicles served in their factory-applied sand finish with distinctive big hull crosses and vehicle numbers on both the hull and turret. Camouflaged vehicles at this time were rare in 502, making my subject vehicle with its brush-painted camouflage especially unusual. This vehicle fitted all my modelling criteria: no Feifel filters fitted, although the trunking on the engine deck remains; turret track brackets fitted, but no roof periscope; 'S' mines are fitted, which I would have preferred to avoid; and the turret smoke grenades, which were being removed at this time, also remain. The vehicle is also seen without the outer first roadwheel, which it was common practice to remove when operating in muddy conditions.

The build

I followed the kit assembly instructions through to stage 12 although I left off any small details and hull fittings and I removed the front mudflaps as these would be replaced by the more detailed Aber versions. Stage 12 covers the assembly of the roadwheels with their separate rubber tyres, and it was necessary to modify a pair of front wheels – roadwheel A in the kit instructions – so that they lack the outer wheel rim. With the wheels all fitted and the top deck temporarily in place the basic hull assembly was complete and I moved on to the turret.

Once again I followed the kit instruction for the assembly of the turret, taking care to get a good clean joint on the gun barrel and muzzle brake, which were filled and sanded with fine-grade abrasive cloth to bring them to a polished finish. Even during the basic assembly it was necessary to add some details like the three sets of recessed grub screws on the barrel sleeve. These holes were drilled and I made tiny screw heads by engraving a slot in some plastic sheet, which I then centred in a punch and die and knocked out. These were then fitted in the holes. I also added the three-part strip that fits on the front of the turret roof behind the mantlet. The tricky part here was making the six recessed hexagonal screw fittings that hold the strips in place. I used a hexagonal punch without the die to emboss a hexagonal hole into some plastic before placing it into a larger-sized hole in my round punch and die and knocking out the circle with the hexagonal rebate centred in it. It took a few attempts but I soon had the six fasteners I required. My final modification to the turret at this stage was to enhance the cast texture on areas of the mantlet by applying Mr Surfacer, which was stippled and then sanded back.

The modified front roadwheel with its outer rim removed.

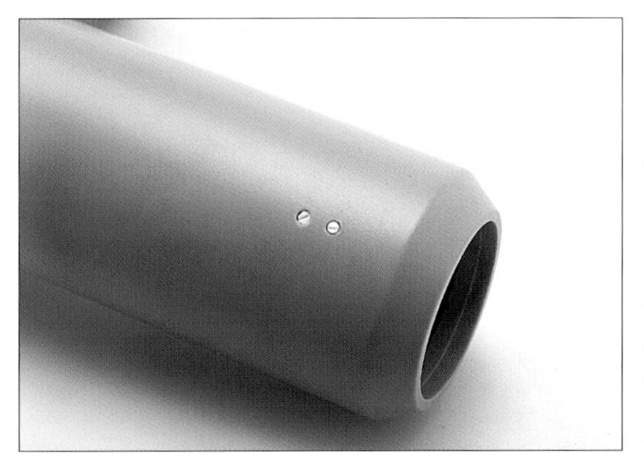

Grub screws are added to the gun sleeve.

This three-part strip where the turret roof joins the mantlet is missing from the kit.

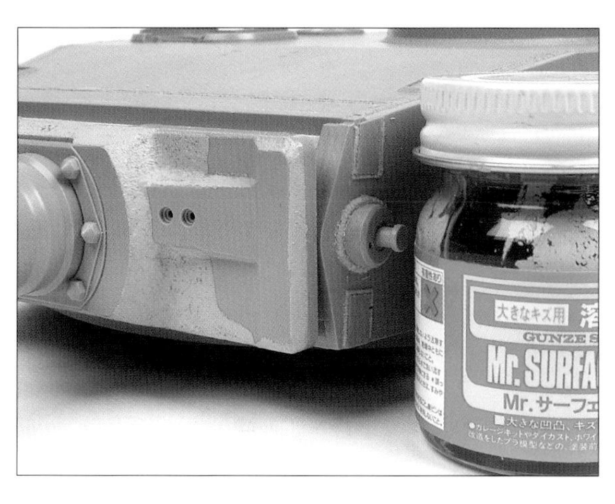

The texture of the mantlet is reworked with some coats of Mr Surfacer stippled on with a brush.

The textured surface is rubbed down to give a cast appearance.

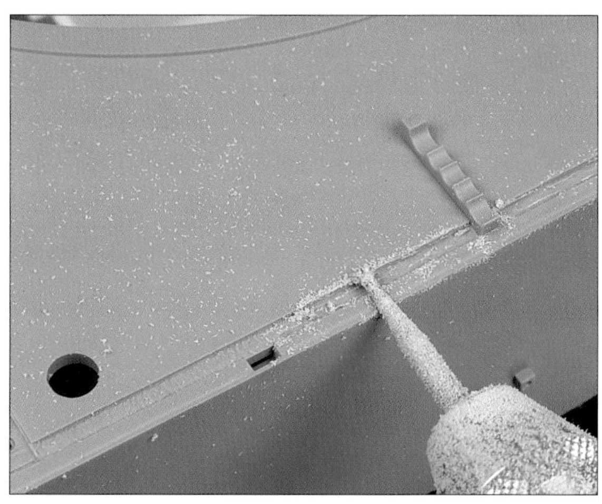

A mini drill with a burr is used to remove the moulded kit weld seams

Using the homemade tool, an irregular pattern is pressed in to the putty.

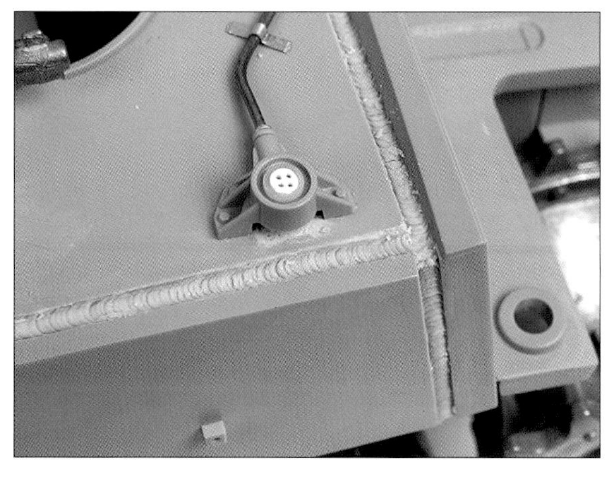

Any excess can be cleaned off when it dries leaving this finished effect.

With the basic assembly completed my next task was to replace all the weld beads on the hull and turret as the kit weld beads were not convincing and there were joints running across some of them. This turned out to be a time-consuming job. I used a mini drill with a router head to rebate the main hull and turret weld beads. When this was done I applied new beads using Magic Sculpt epoxy putty. The putty was forced roughly into the rebate and then textured using a selection of different-sized homemade tools made from brass tube. Using a repetitive prodding action with the tool produced an arc-shaped ridged pattern, which was then brushed over with a wet brush that softened the pattern and blurred any hard edges and, as the putty began to harden, any surplus was easily removed. To check the finish and seal all my welds I applied a coat of Mr Surfacer 1000 once they had dried.

Staying with the turret I began to work on the turret bin. The Tamiya kit has moulded-on lids that I cut away so I could replace these with the Aber versions, which can be made to open in true Aber style although mine would be fixed in place. Time for a word about working with the Aber set. I used soldering whenever possible when working with this because of the added strength it gives. The set is a masterpiece and adds so many fine details that help lift the finished model, but there are always times when you must stand back and ask if folding sheet metal is the best way to get the end result you want and just because it is on the fret does not mean that you must use it. For example, on the turret bin lids, rather than roll the hinges I cut my own from brass tube, which saved a good deal of fiddly work. New rivet detail was applied along the top edge of the bin with plastic rivets which I made by embossing a point into a sheet of plastic and then trimming off the resulting domes. The latches are from the Aber set and, because I did not need them to open, I saved myself time by soldering them together rather than adding the pins.

The spare track brackets for the turret sides are supplied with the Aber set as solid brass parts and a useful template is also included to help position them. I joined the hinged elements with plastic rod hinges with the ends heated to prevent them falling out, and once they were fitted to the turret I added weld beads around all the fittings. The commander's cupola needed only minor modifications with a new spring mechanism made from fuse wire, the drain holes around the rim were filled and re-drilled, weld detail was added to the hatch rest and. these features, together with the latch that holds open the hatch, all came from the Aber set. The loader's hatch with its four-point locking mechanism is ripe for an Aber rework and, sure enough, their set provides all the parts needed to make the mechanism operate. I discarded Aber's version of the small latch at the top of the hatch and shaped my own from plastic.

Finally on the turret I tackled the smoke grenade racks. I began by hollowing out the grenade tubes with a burr on a mini drill as they are only slightly rebated. Aber supply all the detail for the back of the base plate with screw fixings, electrical connectors and tiny chains, and, with these assembled and fitted, the fun really began as I attempted to fit the three electrical cables inside a plastic rod conduit that locates via a small clasp on the central base plate and then snakes its way up the bracket to locate on the roof. A considerable number of test fittings were required in order to get everything aligned, but at last I managed it and the base plate was fixed onto the mounting bracket. In order to align the two bolts that hold the base plate in place I drilled through the bracket and fitted the Aber bolts (which are folded from flat sheet of course) over plastic rods inserted in the holes and then trimmed the rod to the required length.

With the turret assembly completed I returned to work on the hull and began by assembling the front and rear mudflaps, which are ideal for fabrication from photo-etched sheets. These are simple enough to assemble and even the big side hinges are of such a size that getting them to interlock convincingly is quite easy. However, the row of top pivots on the front flaps are

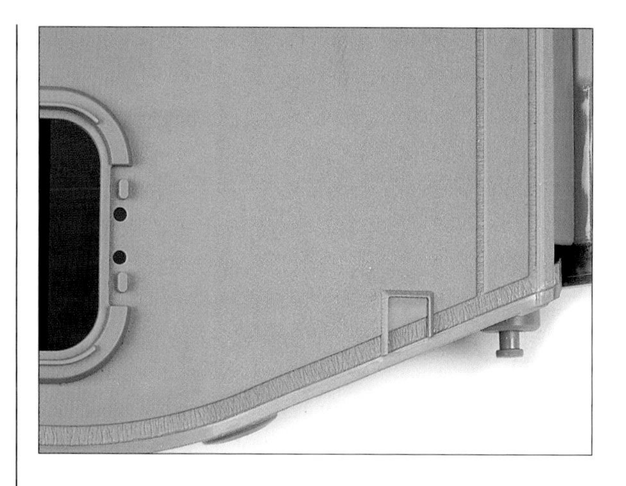

The turret roof welds before …

… and after having the weld detail reworked.

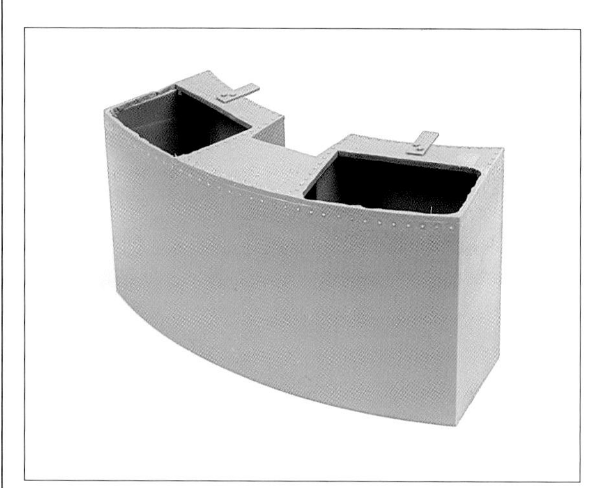

The turret bin with its lids cut away and the tiny rivet detail around the top applied.

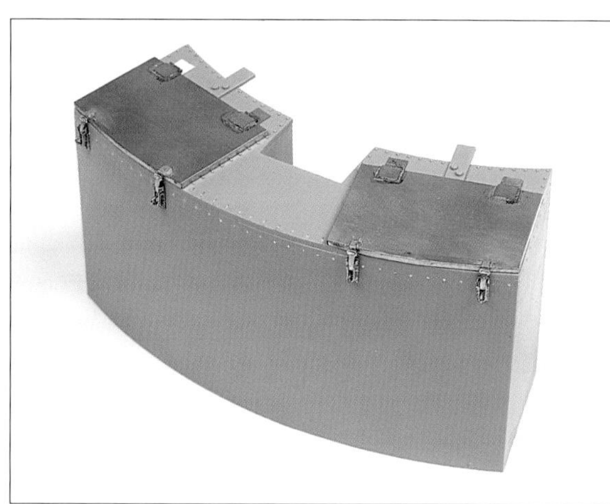

The finished bin with the Aber lids and latches fitted.

A close-up of the latch detail on the bin.

The solid-brass track holders are part of the Aber detail set. Plastic rod was used as a hinge with the ends heated to stop them coming apart.

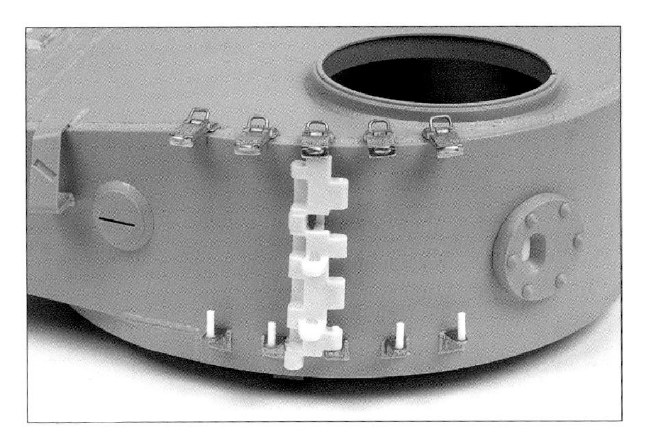

The track holders fitted to the turret. The bottom section already has weld detail applied in this picture.

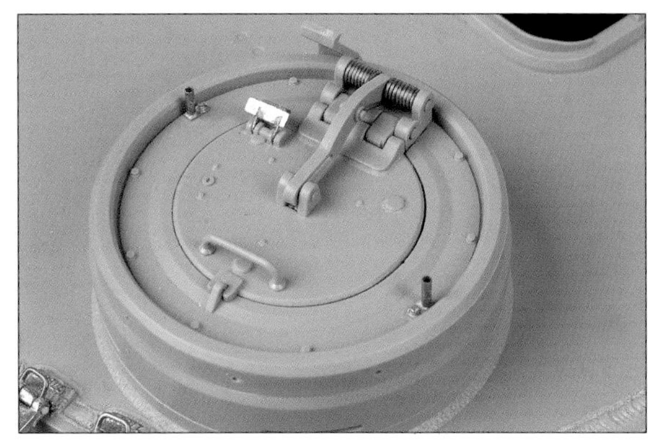

The completed commander's cupola.

Detailed additions are confined to the inside of the loader's hatch, where it is possible make a working locking mechanism, but this one remains fixed.

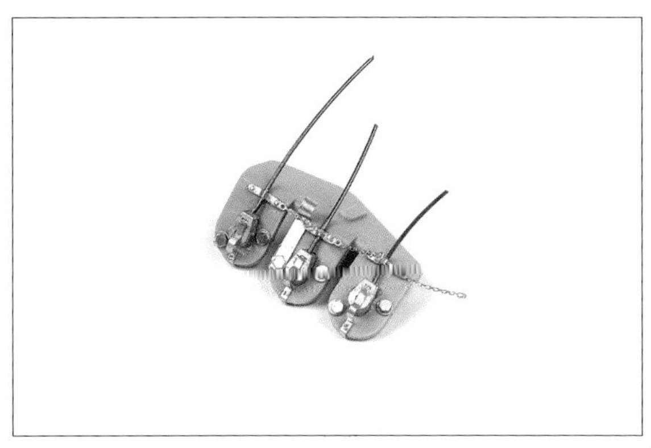

The base plate for the smoke grenades with the fixings and electrical connections from the Aber set.

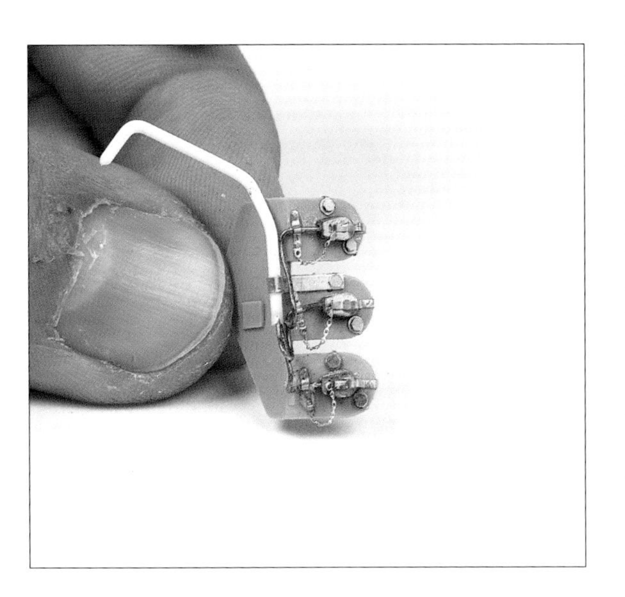

Plumbing the electrics into the conduit and getting the whole assembly to line up with the turret roof was difficult.

Part of the problem is the awkward position of these delicate details. Two lengths of plastic rod serve to align the mounting bolts for the base plate.

The tubes were drilled out before fitting.

One of the Aber front mudflaps nearing completion.

The Tamiya tracks with their open top face are replaced with the superior S&T individual-link resin tracks.

A detail of the cast texture applied to the exhaust covers. Notice also the weld detail applied using Green Stuff before switching to Magic Sculpt.

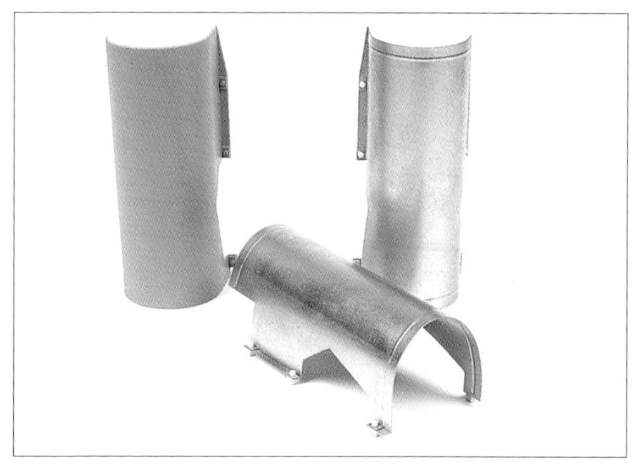

The kit exhaust shroud has no ribs around each end so Aber provides a solution.

tricky and I chose to fit mine to the flaps rather than the hull as the instructions suggest as I knew they would never line up otherwise. I also found one of the gaps for the pivot just too small so I had to make a narrower version in plastic so that it would fit. Both sets of mudflaps were left separate to help with fitting the tracks later. Talking of the tracks, the kit tracks are really not suitable as they have an open upper face that shows the track pin; they also lack the hollow guide horn. Fortunately S&T Productions now produce an individual resin track link that corrects these mistakes and simply clips together so I switched to these.

On the hull rear I began by reworking the exhaust system using parts from the Aber set along with my own plastic parts to detail the exhaust pipe covers that I fitted in the open position consistent with a vehicle that was running. I also applied a textured finish to the exhaust pipes and an even heavier texture to the big cast covers. The sheet metal shrouds in the kit lack the embossed rib around the top and bottom edges but Aber came to the rescue with a set of replacements. Don't use the Aber mounting bolts as they are oversized; I made new ones with a punch and die.

With my vehicle not having any track guards fitted I only had to detail the mounting points down the hull side with weld beads and by drilling out the holes in each one. I nearly missed the fact that the foremost point on each side of the hull has been missed off the kit and I had to make a new one. One other minor detail was to bevel the top edge of each mounting point. The left side of the hull is festooned with mounting brackets for the track changing rope. The 'U'-shaped brackets are easy enough to form from the Aber set but the five clamps are much more demanding. For all the Aber clamp fittings on the kit I dispensed with their representation of screw-threaded rods, which are two dimensional, and replaced them with brass rod. The clamps are complex to assemble, especially if you want them to operate so that you can insert tools later, but with so many to make you do develop a technique with them. I used the kit track rope as a guide for locating all the brackets and Aber supply some superb braided-steel wire for the rope itself. It is a bit of a handful to fit and I found some Blu-Tack useful for holding sections in place.

On the front of the hull there were only minor changes to make with new wing nut clamps added either side of the machine-gun ball mount. On this occasion I had some small brass bolts of the correct size to allow me to add proper threaded rods.

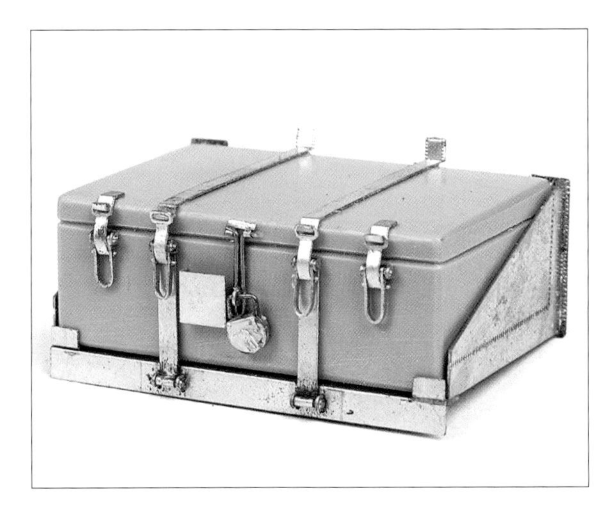

Almost a stand-alone model. The reworked toolbox even has a padlock.

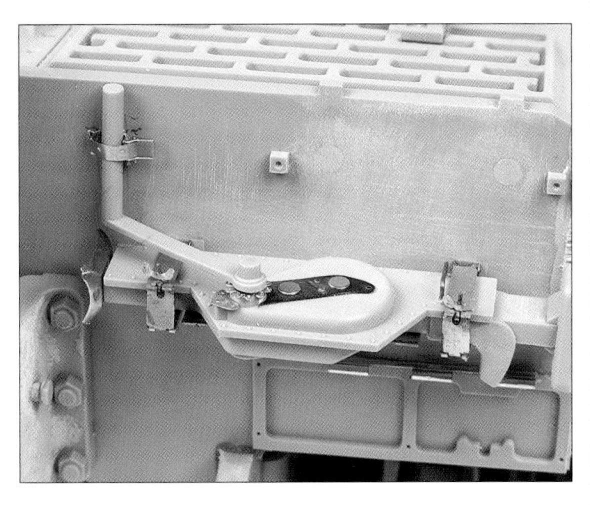

The complex pivoting clamps for the jack are mostly hidden when it is fitted. The weld beads on the mounting blocks have yet to be added.

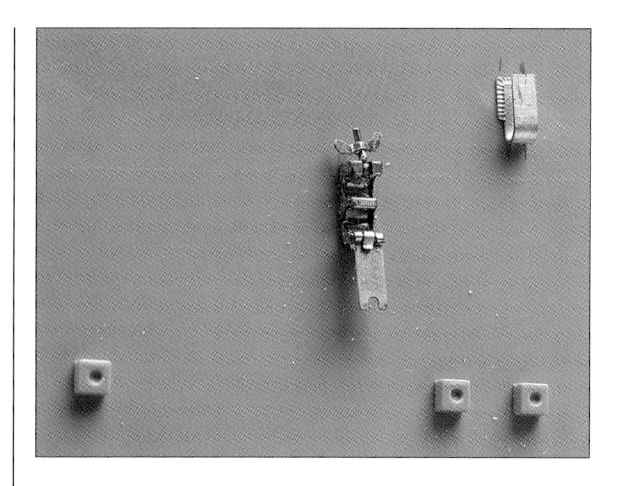

The tiny Aber clasps to hold the track rope in place: note the etched-effect weld bead.

New weld beads were applied to the hull fittings – here the mounting blocks are done but not the clasp.

Fitting the metal track cable is tricky and Blu-Tack helps hold the cable in place.

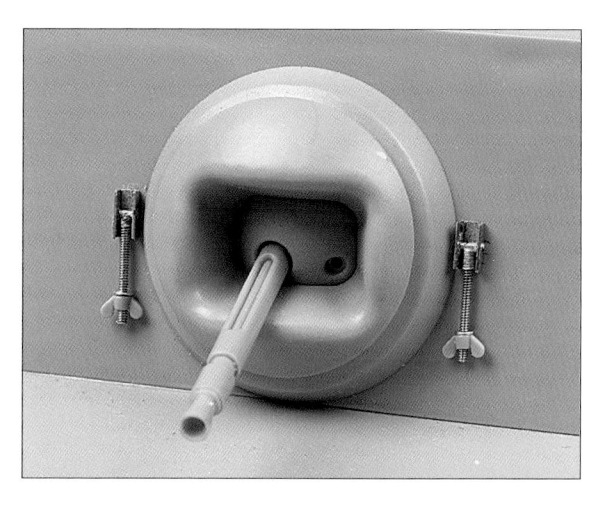

Real screw threads were used for the waterproof cover clamps.

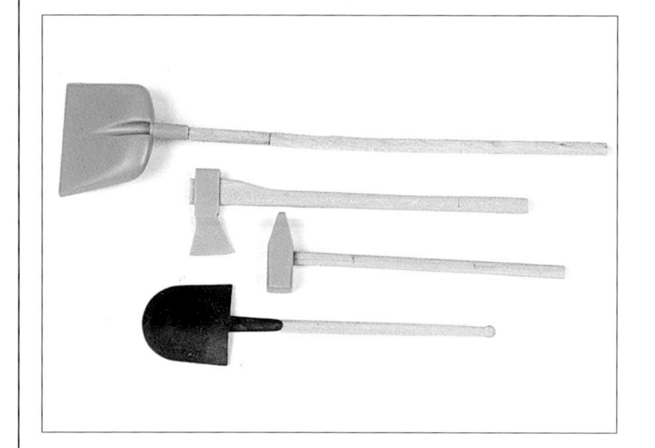

The kit tool handles were removed and replaced with new wooden versions mostly made from cocktail sticks.

Cocktail sticks were just the right size for the gun cleaning rods. Sections of screw thread with brass tube were used to make the screw-together caps.

Two views of the reworked fire extinguisher.

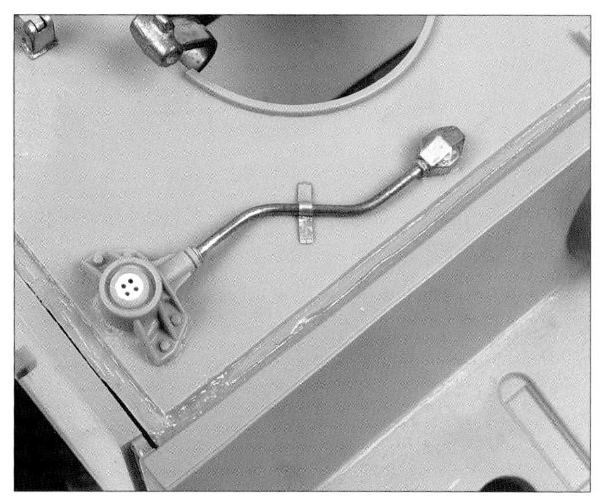

The headlamp fitting showing the four-pin socket and new cable connection.

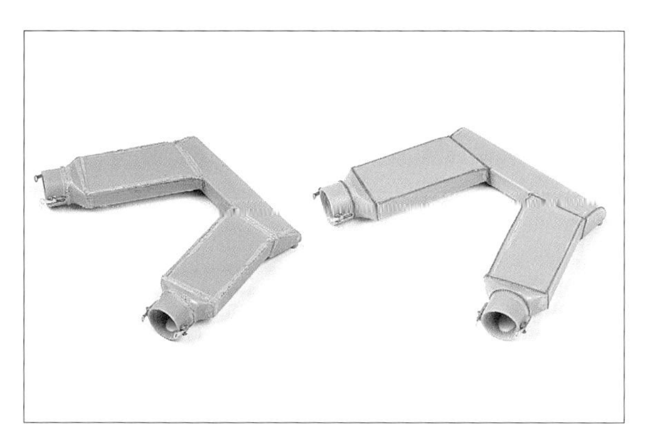

Two attempts at the weld detail on the trunking. On the left is the first one, which was replaced with the more delicate plastic rod version on the right.

The engine deck hatch with screw-threaded posts to hold the hoses of the air filter system.

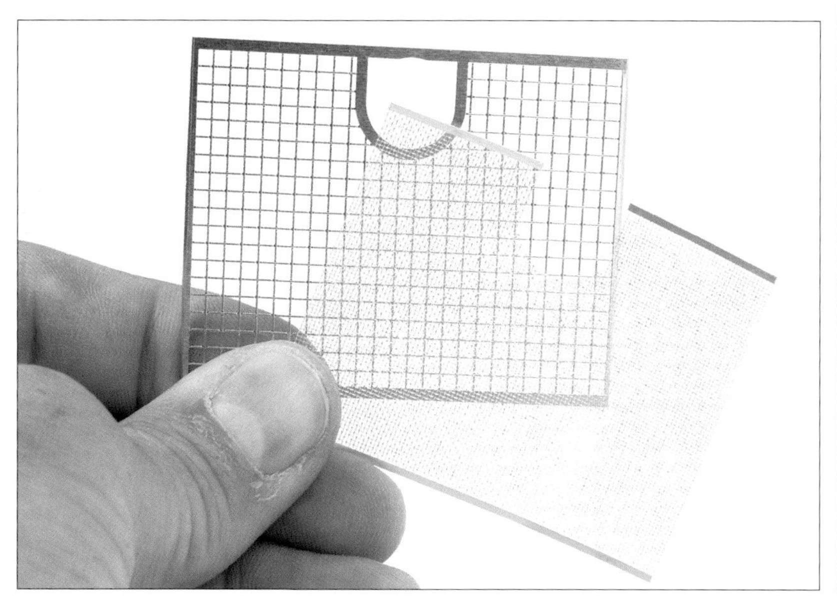

The Aber-supplied engine deck screen with the silver finish seen here with additional mesh from the Aber range.

All the screens fitted to the engine deck.

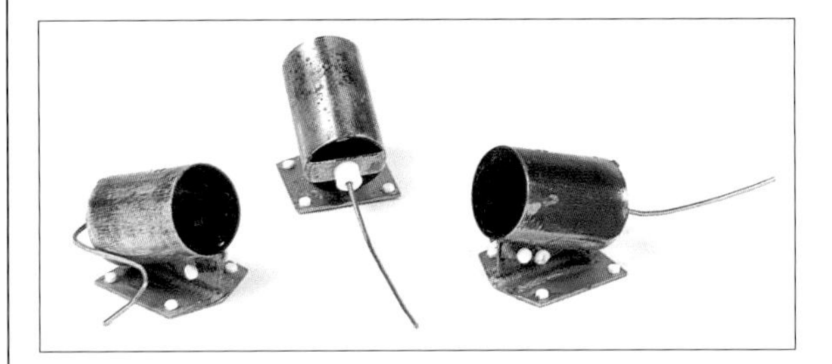

The completed hull-mounted 'S' mine launchers, all formed from flat sheet.

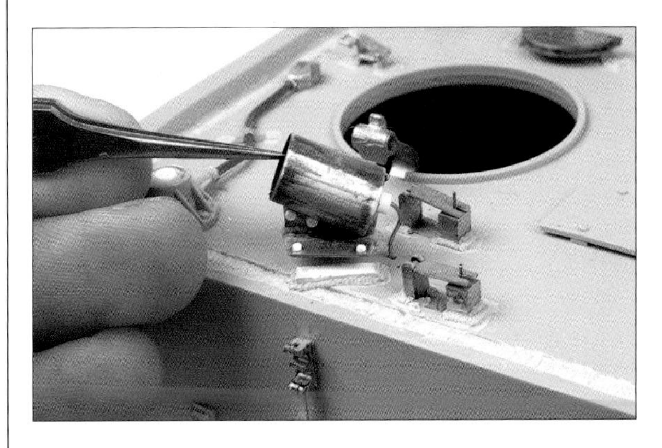

Fitting one of the front launchers: note the new mounting brackets and the firing cable feeding through the hull roof.

The inside of one of the front hatches with the new Aber locking mechanism. The periscope is not fitted at this stage.

Moving to the upper deck I began by reworking the vehicle tools and I decided to replace all the handles with new wooden versions. With the exception of the axe handle these were all made from cocktail sticks that were shaped using the plastic examples as a guide. The long shovel handle was made from two sticks joined together and bent using steam to soften the wood. I positioned the join where one of the clamps would hold so this would be hidden. The gun cleaning rods also used cocktail sticks with brass tube collars at each end and a brass screw thread fitted for that finishing touch.

Moving to the engine deck, my first task was to add a cast texture and casting number to the snorkel cover. Although the Feifel system had been removed from my subject vehicle the well-known photo of it with its engine deck cover open showed that the intake trunking remained fitted to the cover. This was a sheet metal assembly and I added the weld detail to all the edges using the same techniques as before. I also had to drill out the ends where the hoses would connect and blank off the underside, which then became visible. Having completed the weld detail I was unhappy with the finished effect – the weld beads were just too big so they had to go. I replaced them with thin plastic rod, which received several coats of liquid glue until the plastic distorted to a realistic bobbly weld pattern. The posts for the Feifel hose clamps needed some attention and I wanted to add a screw thread to the top section of each. Soldering the sections of screw thread onto lengths of brass tube so that they looked straight proved to be more difficult than I expected but eventually I had the four that I needed and I fitted them with their requisite weld detail.

The engine deck intakes need to be covered with their protective mesh screens, which fortunately Aber supplies. In reality these screens were made of two grades of mesh, something which is visible in this scale and not covered by the Aber update set which only gives the bigger outer mesh, so I selected another suitable mesh from the Aber range and spot soldered it behind the bigger-grade upgrade parts. Next I had to add the 'S' mine throwers that my vehicle sported, and that Tamiya overlooked, only moulding the mounting plates on the hull, although even they are too shallow so I had to remove them and add deeper versions. Luckily, Aber has this covered with a complete set of the throwers, which proved to be very difficult to fabricate. To begin with the tubes themselves have to be rolled from flat sheet, which is not easy, but eventually I had them assembled. The rear corner versions also have to have mounting brackets assembled but after the launchers themselves these make for light relief. I could find no reference for the wiring connection at the back of the launcher so I took a guess with some plastic tube and drilled holes in the hull roof to feed the cables into.

The pair of front hull hatches is a complete model in itself courtesy of the Aber upgrade set. Aber also provides a working locking mechanism that looks superb when it is all assembled with even tiny castellated nuts, and I added the rubber seal around the inside edge of the hatch with plastic rod. The periscopes are another superbly complex Aber component. I decided to make perspex lenses for the vision blocks to slide inside the Aber metal cases. I replaced the periscope frames with my own made from plastic as the Aber ones did not look correct. These then have to hinge in order to insert the lenses, which caused me some problems. I knew that gluing the hinges to the frames would not be strong enough so I soldered them onto some thin brass sheet, which was then glued to the frames – it was a small cheat but given the problems of getting all these free-floating components to line up correctly I thought it was acceptable. I made the small springs for the side of the frame from thin brass wire wound around a drill bit.

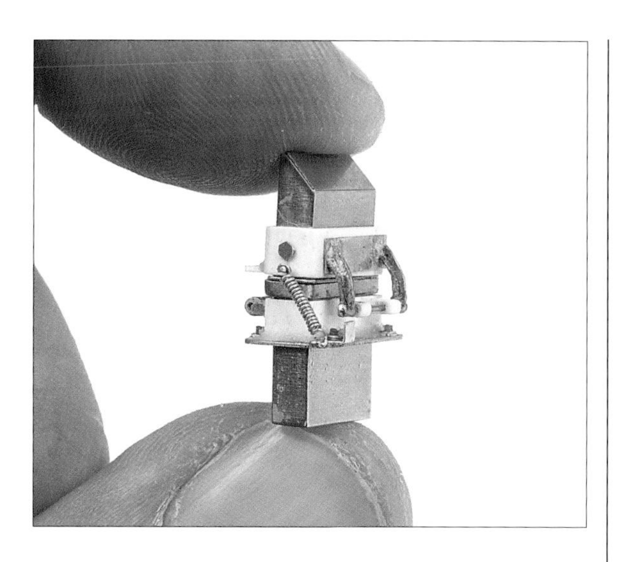

The complex Aber periscope assembly with some of my own modifications.

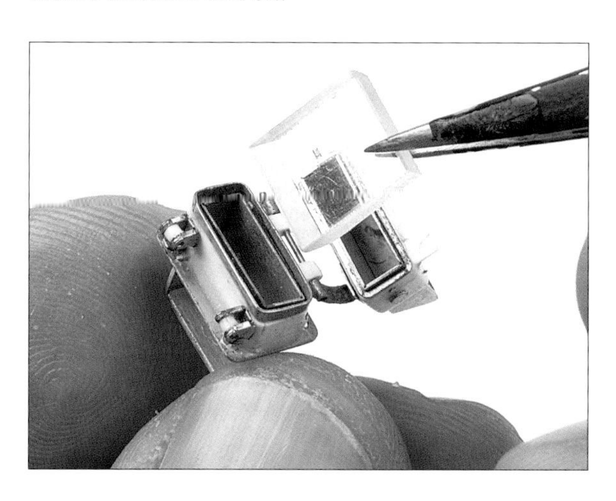

The empty periscope cases were begging to be filled, so I made my own lenses from Perspex.

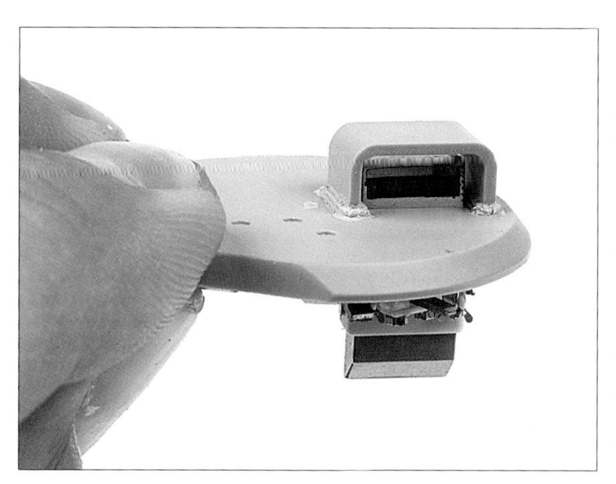

Weld-bead detail completes the outside of the hatch.

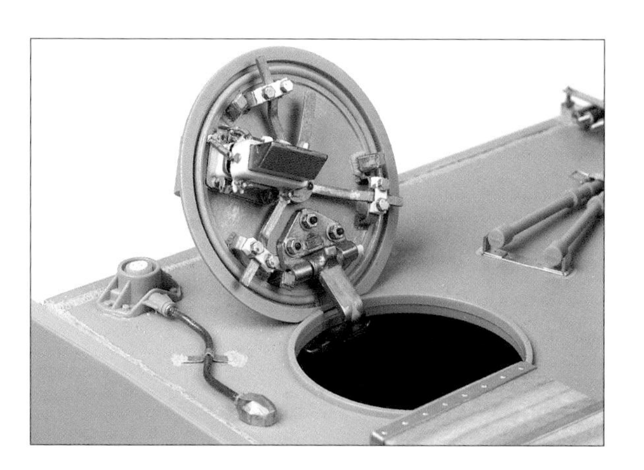

The finished hatch is temporarily mounted on the hinge with a plastic pin.

The assembly is completed and all the fittings are in place.

ABOVE A front view of the completed model.

ABOVE A rear view of the completed model ready for paint.

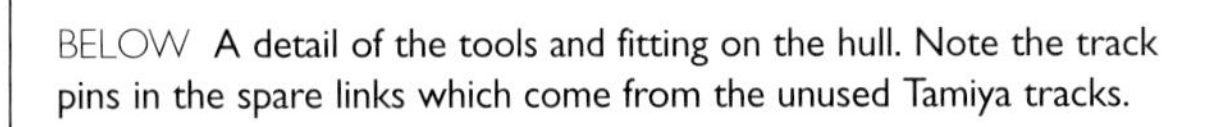

BELOW A detail of the tools and fitting on the hull. Note the track pins in the spare links which come from the unused Tamiya tracks.

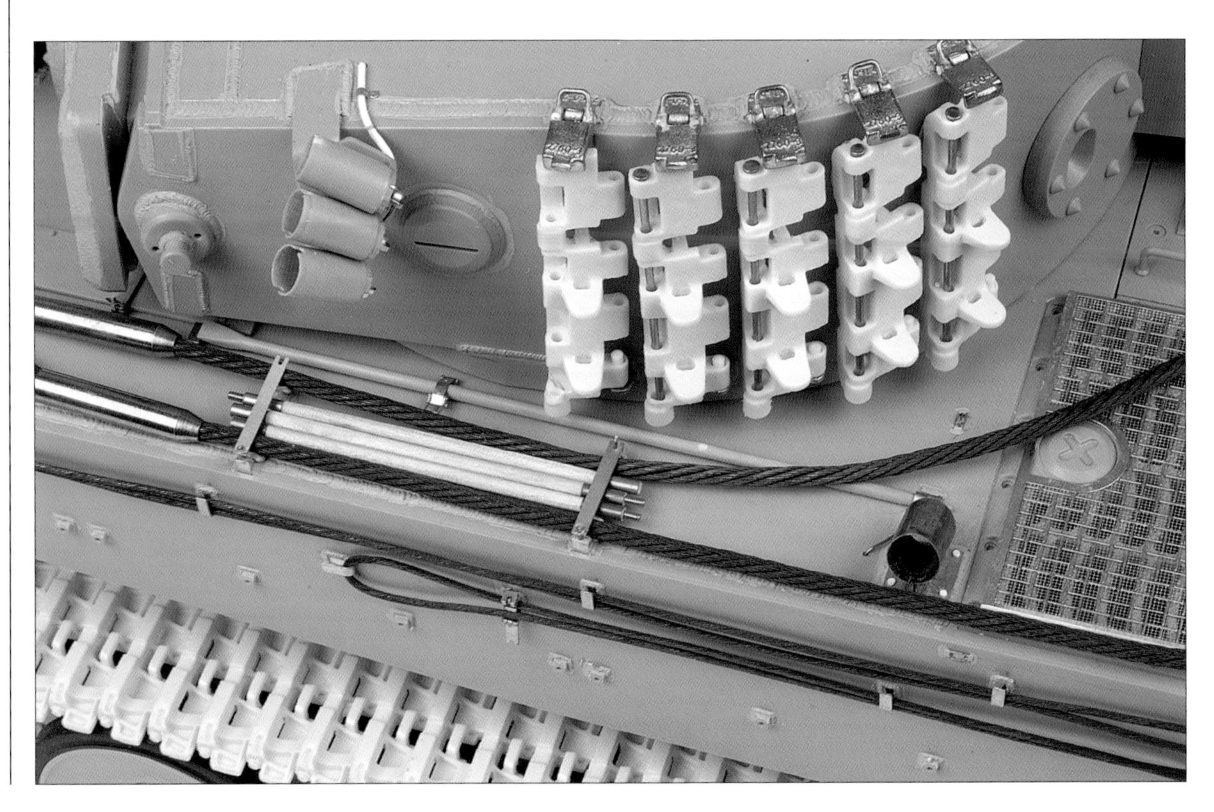

Painting

I stripped down the model for painting, removing the gun barrel, wheels, tracks, hatches and all the tools and cables, and I applied a basecoat of sand yellow using Humbrol enamels. The numbers and national markings were all hand painted along with the 502 elephant logo on the glacis, and with five sets of numbers to apply it took considerable control to keep them all looking the same. Next came the challenge of the camouflage, which was easy in some areas where I had good photographic reference and pure guesswork in others. From what I could see the engine deck showed no sign of any camouflage, yet the cupola was striped and I supposed the turret roof would be also but I decided not to apply any camo to the upper hull deck or hull rear. I mixed my own tone of green enamel and began by copying the areas that I could see in the photos. It took me three evenings' work to apply the camouflage with gritted teeth as it looked so stark and just wrong – I was desperate to spray a nice soft-edged camouflage pattern! I did indeed get out the airbrush to apply a coat of satin varnish followed by a dusting of Humbrol No. 72 as a dry dirt colour over the lower hull and on some of the upper surfaces. This was followed by a dark grey-brown wash over the whole vehicle. This allowed me to add some staining down the vertical surfaces and on areas like behind the spare tracks on the turret sides. I followed this up by airbrushing a diluted brown-black mix into all the crevices and recess and around the turret ring. I began to add areas of wear to the paintwork, for example around the hatches, the edges of the turret and the bow. Small chips and scratches were applied in a red oxide primer colour using a fine brush and then the process was repeated using a dark-brown mix for areas of especially heavy wear. The edges of the turret and the hatches were also burnished with some silver foil to give a polished finish.

I now turned to painting the tools and smaller fittings. Because I had used wood for all the handles of the tools I simply enhanced what was already there by painting some subtle woodgrain using very diluted blacks and browns. The metal parts were finished in Mr Metal Color buffable steel, whilst the brass parts of the gun cleaning rods were left unpainted with just the screw threads and plastic inserts touched in with Mr Metal Color Brass. The spare track links and tow cable were finished in various tones of grey and brown and washed in some lighter grey shades, and some rust stains were added here and there. The tracks were sprayed with a dark chocolate-brown enamel and then the treads were given a coat of Mr Metal Color, which was polished once it had dried. The exhausts were painted in a pinky rust shade before adding clusters of darker rust spots with a fine brush. As only the top would eventually be visible I did

With a basecoat of sand applied all the markings were painted by hand.

The result looks very stark but it is ready to be camouflaged.

It looks even worse with the camouflage applied, so it is important not to lose your nerve at this point.

An overspray of dirt tones it down although with hindsight this application was probably a bit heavy.

A dark wash improves the look and picks out details.

not worry about finishing the lower parts. For the soot staining I decided to apply black pastel with an old brush rather than risk spraying and have the black hit areas I wanted to be clean; I applied this only to the exhaust stacks. When this was complete I used a Post-It note to mask the stacks while I sprayed the back and top of the hull and the inside of the exhaust shrouds.

LEFT A very diluted dark-brown shade is sprayed to darken shadow areas.

BELOW This is how things looked after the shading with the airbrush.

Small paint chips are added to the front of the hull where the crew normally mount the vehicle.

The tools are painted using Mr Metal Color buffable paint for the steel parts.

Subtle woodgrain is applied to the handles.

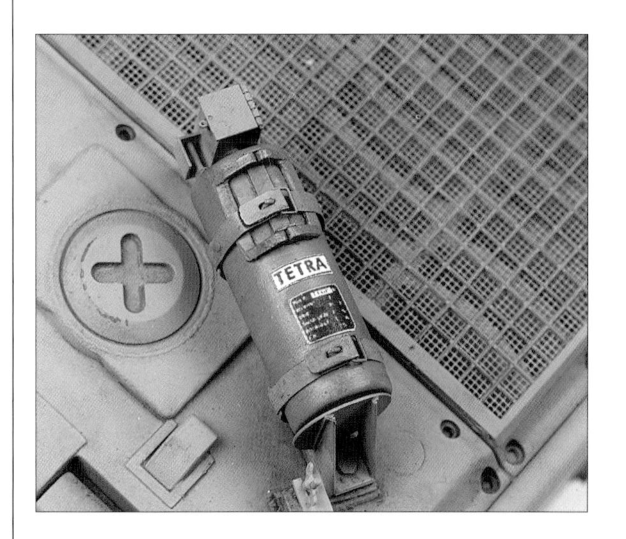

Computer-generated labels are the finishing touch for the fire extinguisher

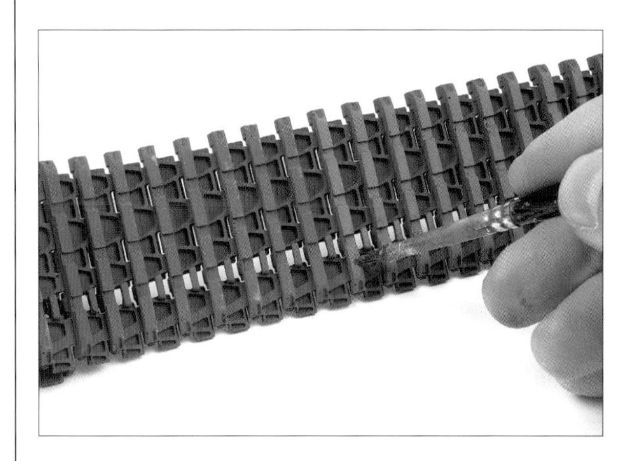

A brown basecoat on the tracks is followed by a highlight of Mr Metal Color.

Overlaid colours and a subtle metallic shine complete the spare track links.

Once it has dried it is polished to a shine.

Getting dirty

Finally it was time to apply the mud. I spent some time experimenting with different tones of pigments to get a wet and dry tone that I was happy with. My mud mix was made from pigments or powdered pastels mixed with matt or satin acrylic varnish and a little PVA glue. I applied the dry areas first using an old brush to stipple the mix and give a mud texture. I used the same techniques with the wet darker colour, applying a thick mix to the rear of the hull sides and gradually thinning it out as the mud thinned towards the front of the hull. For the especially muddy areas I added some fine sand and static grass into the mix to thicken it up. For the roadwheels I applied a very dilute mud mix to each before fitting each wheel in my mini drill and spinning it to disperse the mud in a realistic radial pattern. I then repeated this process but with my normal thick mud mix which produced a finish that seemed to replicate very closely the finish in the photos. To blend in other areas like the engine decks, where mud is thrown up onto them by the tracks, I used a stiff bristle brush to flick and splatter areas of mud. Areas of wet staining were added using a very diluted mix of mud with matt or satin varnish and oil stains were applied around the filler caps on the engine deck.

Finishing touches

One of my final tasks was to complete the front hatches by painting and fitting the periscopes. The locking mechanism was finished using Vallejo Black, which has a slight sheen finish, and this was then given a wash of pastels. The periscope cases were painted in a dark brown to replicate their Bakelite finish and for the ultimate in realism I applied a coat of special mirror paint to the angled parts of the actual lenses. I added some spare track pins to the links on the turret using those supplied with the Tamiya tracks which had a stainless steel finish. I gave them a subtle rusty wash to tone them down and glued them in place. Finally I added the rear convoy light that I had made from clear plastic. This was coloured using blue felt pens and spattered slightly with mud to blend in.

The first stage of painting the exhausts with the spotted darker tones over the pinky base colour.

Black soot stains are applied using pastels.

The exhausts are masked and the hull is sprayed with more black stains.

The shrouds are fitted showing the exhaust stains leaking realistically around the edges.

A dried mud mix of pastels, PVA glue and varnish is stippled onto the hull. The wet mix is then applied over the top.

The wet mix is then applied over the top.

The density is decreased as it moves to the front of the hull.

Static grass and sand are used to thicken the mud in certain areas.

Mud splatters across the engine deck.

Darker streaks of moisture run down the hull panels.

The texture of the mud adds to the realistic finish and note the spatters up the 'S' mine launcher.

For ultimate realism, mirror finish paint is applied to the angled faces of the periscopes.

The rear convoy light sits under the toolbox.

323

323

Kits available

1/35-scale kits

Tamiya Tiger Ausf. E (Late) TM35146
Tamiya Tiger I Mid Production TM35194
Tamiya Tiger I Mid Production 'Otto Carius' TM35202
Tamiya Tiger I Frühe Production TM35216
Tamiya Tiger I Initial Production (Afrika) TM35227
Academy Tiger IE Early Production with Full Interior AC1348
Academy German Tiger IE (Early Version – No Interior) AC1386
Academy Tiger IE Mid Production with Full Interior AC1387
AFV Club German Tiger IE Heavy Tank (Late Production) AFV35079
AFV Club Tiger I Late Version Heavy Tank 'Michael Wittmann Special' AFV35S27
DML Pz.Kpfw. VI Ausf. E (Sd.Kfz. 181) Tiger I Initial Type (3 in 1) 6252
DML Tiger I Late Production (3 in 1), Pz.Kpfw. VI Ausf. E – Sd.Kfz. 181 6253

1/48-scale kits

Tamiya German Tiger IE (Early Production) Heavy Tank TM32504
Tamiya 1/48 German Tiger I Initial Production (Afrika-Korps) TM32529
Skybow German Tiger IE (Early Production) SKY4833

1/16-scale kits

Tamiya 1/16 Tiger I Heavy Tank Full-Option R/C TM56010

Tamiya's Initial Tiger I can be built to represent a version used in North Africa.

Optional parts included with the 'Frühe' Tamiya kit allows it to be built into one of several configurations.

DML's Tiger I Late Production was released in 2005, and included many optional parts previously available only as aftermarket accessories.

The Deutsche Afrika Korps (DAK) Tiger I was released as a limited production run by DML's on-line business Cyber-Hobby.

Further reading, media and websites

Books

Building an accurate model of the Tiger I tank involves consulting reference material. It would be difficult to name all of the references available at this time on such a popular subject as the Tiger I, so the following list of books is a summary of the most useful references to the modeller, and how valuable they were to aid some of the projects in this title.

Bitoh, Mitsuru, *et al.*, Achtung Panzer 6: *PanzerKampfwagen Tiger* Dai Nippon Kaiga Publishing: Tokyo, 1999

This book from the Achtung Panzer series includes detail drawings and informative photos of a very high standard. The volume covers all of the vehicles under the name 'Tiger', including the Königstiger, Ferdinand, Elefant, Sturmtiger and Jagdtiger. The amount of information on the Tiger I is sparse compared to the in-depth coverage given other vehicles in this series of books.

Creighton, Angus, *How to Build Tamiya's Steel Wheeled Tiger I* ADH Publishing: Totternhoe, 2001

Renowned modeller Angus Creighton shows how to construct five models of Tamiya's 1/35-scale late-production Tiger. This softcover book is full of very useful information to the modeller on detailing the later variants and includes many valuable modelling and painting techniques. Super-detailing, figure conversions and *Zimmerit* application are documented along with a guide on details to note when modelling this vehicle.

Feist, Uwe, and Culver, Bruce, *Tiger I and Sturmtiger in Detail* Ryton Publications: Bellingham, WA, 1994

This hardbound reference is packed with information on the Tiger I, with top-quality museum and period photos. The Sturmtiger is also covered in a similar fashion.

Hernandez Cabos, Rodrico, Osprey Modelling Manuals 13: *Panzerkampfwagen VI Tiger* Osprey Publishing: Oxford, 2001

Not to be confused with the Osprey Modelling Series, this book was one of a different series of books compiled with some material from the Spanish modelling magazine *EuroModelisimo*. Examples of excellent modelling techniques combined with superb photography make this an attractive and inspiring guide to modelling the Tiger I. An in-depth article on a super-detailed Sturmtiger is also featured, along with museum reference pictures of the late-production Tiger I in Saumur.

Jentz, Thomas L., and Doyle, Hilary L., New Vanguard 5: *Tiger I Heavy Tank 1942–45* Osprey Publishing Ltd: Oxford, 1993

Technical information on the Tiger I tank is summed up in this publication from the well-established series by Osprey. This affordable title contains a condensed version of the more elaborate *D.W. to Tiger I* title by the same pair of authors.

Jentz, Thomas L., and Doyle, Hilary L., *Germany's Tiger Tanks D.W. to Tiger I: Design, Production & Modifications* Schiffer Publishing Ltd: Atglen, PA, 2000

This large-format hardcover book is clearly the best reference on the subject to date. The research information, photos, drawings and modification charts contained in the 190 pages are an extremely good guide to building an accurate and authentic model.

Jentz, Thomas L., *Germany's Tiger Tanks Tigers at the Front* Schiffer Publishing Ltd: Atglen, PA, 2001
This title consists of a photographic compilation of the Tiger I and II throughout their entire production run. The selection of pictures and thoroughly researched captions make this a valuable addition to the modeller's reference collection.
Restayn, Jean, *Tiger I on the Eastern Front* Histoire et Collections: Paris, 1999
The first of two books by Jean Restayn has many photos and colour plates of Tiger units on the Russian front. Geared for modellers, it is a popular reference for Tiger I enthusiasts.
Restayn, Jean, *Tiger I on the Western Front* Histoire et Collections, Paris, 2001
Completing the two hardbound volume series, this title covers the Tigers that fought on the Western Front.
Schneider, Wolfgang, *Tigers In Combat I* J.J. Fedorowicz Publishing: Winnipeg, 1994
One of the biggest collections of photos published in a large hardcover volume, this title chronicles the unit histories of the heavy tank battalions of the *Heer*. The abundance of photographs provides many detail and marking references. Out of print for a few years, popular demand brought it back to the shelves.
Schneider, Wolfgang, *Tigers in Combat II* J.J. Fedorowicz Publishing: Winnipeg, 1998
As a follow up to *Tigers in Combat I*, this book covers the Waffen SS and Grossdeutschland heavy tank units. It was used frequently when researching the Wittmann 13./SS Panzer Regiment 1 '1331' and s.SS.Pz.Abt.101 '321' models in this book.
Stansell, Patrick A., *The Modeler's Guide To The Tiger Tank* Ampersand Publishing Co. Inc.: Delray Beach, FL, 2003
Covering both the Tiger I and Tiger II tanks, *Military Miniatures In Review* editor Pat Stansell has pieced together a very comprehensive guide to modelling these vehicles that includes 13 completed 1/35-scale kits. There is a wealth of detailed drawings and period photographs showing all aspects of the Tigers from the initial trail version to the final vehicles produced in late 1944. The book also contains an excellent guide to the purchase and application of many modelling accessories to detail the available kits.

Websites

www.tiger1.info is an informational website on the Tiger I created and maintained by David Byrden. It is a wealth of reference for the modeller and includes drawings and photographs not published elsewhere. There also is a continually updated list of corrections to some of the available Tiger I model kits.

www.missing-lynx.com is an extremely well-populated website devoted to all AFV modeling with model gallery, numerous discussion groups, and useful links. Other popular sites include www.armorama.com, www.planetarmor.com and www.track-link.net.

www.achtungpanzer.com has a good write-up on the history of the Tiger I and the units it served in, along with photos, videos and veterans' accounts of wartime experiences.

Index